Evolving Societal Norms

From Survival Instincts to Civilized Behaviors: A Path to Societal Harmony

Joseph Aminian

All Rights Reserved

No part of this book may be reproduced, or stored in a retrieval system, or transmitted in any form or by any means, electronic, mechanical, photocopying, recording, or otherwise, without express written permission of the publisher. The characters and events portrayed in this book are fictitious. Any similarity to real persons, living or dead, is coincidental and not intended by the author.

ISBN (paperback): 978-1-0688522-6-8
ISBN (eBook): 978-1-0688522-7-5
ISBN (PDF): 978-1-0688522-8-2

First Edition Published November 2024

© Copyright 2024 Joseph Aminian

Tabel of Content

INTRODUCTION	10
CHAPTER 1	12
THE IMPERATIVE OF SURVIVAL	12
CHAPTER 2	31
THE ROLE OF STORYTELLING IN HUMAN BEHAVIOR	31
CHAPTER 3	52
THE EVOLUTION OF HUMAN SOCIETIES AND THE AWARENESS OF HUMAN BOUNDARIES	52
CHAPTER 4	72
THE INTERSECTION OF BIOLOGY AND SPIRITUALITY	72
CHAPTER 5	94
THE CONCEPT OF CIVILIZATION	94
CHAPTER 6	113
FOSTERING LOCALIZED GRASSROOTS INITIATIVES	113

CHAPTER 7   124

PATHWAYS TO A UNIFIED HUMAN SOCIETY   124

CHAPTER 8   142

ENVISIONING A COLLABORATIVE, HARMONIOUS GLOBAL SOCIETY   142

REFERENCES   160

Introduction

Discover the transformative journey of humanity, one that weaves survival instincts with cultural evolution, ultimately carving a path toward societal harmony. This book is more than an exploration; it's a roadmap to understanding the forces that shape our individual and collaborative behaviors.

At its core, "Evolving Societal Norms" examines how fundamental survival drives influence every layer of our communities and society, from the world of organized crime to the realms of scientific discovery. With a unique blend of biological, cognitive, psychological and spiritual insights, the book delves into the intersection of instinct and evolved societal conditioning.

Through engaging narratives, it illuminates how storytelling has shaped civilizations, served as a control mechanism, and now calls for rejuvenation in a rapidly changing world.

This compelling work invites you to question long-standing societal structures, redefine narratives, and embrace the profound role of individual conscience and humility in fostering a civil society. Rich with insights into human behavior, spirituality, and the unseen boundaries that define our interactions, "Evolving Societal Norms" offers readers a path to personal growth and societal awareness.

Designed for curious minds, intellectuals, writers, and seekers of self-improvement, this book is a guide for those who yearn to understand—and perhaps even influence—the next chapter in human evolution. Dive in, and reshape your perspective on what it truly means to be a civilized human.

Joseph Aminian

November 4, 2024

Chapter 1
The Imperative of Survival

Survival is an instinct as ancient as life itself, embedded within our DNA. It serves as an unspoken directive, influencing daily decisions and long-term aspirations, often unconsciously. From simple choices, like selecting a meal or planning a commute, to complex strategies for career advancement and social belonging, the drive to survive forms the foundation of human behavior. Gaining insight into this intrinsic drive offers a perspective through which we can better understand individual actions and societal patterns.

The diverse methods people employ to ensure survival vary greatly. A crime boss may turn to intimidation and violence to maintain control and secure safety in their realm. Conversely, intellectuals like Albert Einstein channel this survival instinct into pioneering scientific pursuits. Despite the stark contrast in environments and approaches, both are driven by a fundamental need to confront threats and establish a legacy. This disparity highlights the adaptability of survival mechanisms, shaping behaviors in both constructive and destructive ways.

This chapter explores the complexities of the survival instinct, examining its influence across societal tiers—from criminals to intellectuals. It investigates how primal drives are subtly shaped by societal myths and narratives that help sustain order and cohesion within communities. As we face contemporary challenges, this chapter argues for evolving these narratives to promote human progress while preserving vital social frameworks. By understanding the core role of the survival imperative, we gain valuable insights into crafting policies and narratives that harness these instincts for the greater good.

The Biological Imperative

The survival instinct influences us in ways we may not consciously recognize, impacting every layer of our being, from our most basic needs to our loftiest ambitions. It could even be described as the underlying code that informs our actions and decisions.

Let's start by addressing fundamental human needs—food, shelter, clothing, healthcare, transportation, and recreation. These necessities are not merely commodities; they represent the lifelines that sustain our existence. At the heart of any complex society lies a network of individuals striving to secure these essentials for themselves and their loved ones. Whether it's a farmer cultivating crops, an engineer constructing homes, or a doctor treating illnesses, each person is driven by the critical need to survive and thrive.

In this context, the human brain is most fully activated when driven by survival. Think of how your mind sharpens when faced with an immediate threat or scarcity. Under duress, the brain mobilizes resources, formulates solutions, and exhibits creativity. This resembles scenes in survival films where protagonists devise ingenious ways to overcome obstacles under immense stress. Far from mere dramatic flair, this reflects how our brains operate in survival mode. The survival instinct often produces acts of exceptional resilience and creativity (Gilkey and Kilts, 2023).

To further illustrate, consider the contrasting paths taken by crime bosses and intellectuals like Einstein and Schrödinger. Although their environments and choices differ vastly, both are motivated by a survival imperative.

Crime bosses, in a world where strength is synonymous with survival, often rely on violence and intimidation. In their realm, any sign of vulnerability can endanger their entire operation. The survival imperative drives them toward a life of danger, where they must continually project dominance to preserve their status. This can be likened to an existential calculus, in which survival depends on exerting power and neutralizing threats. Their brains remain in survival mode, though the expression of this drive is distinct (Campana and Varese, 2023).

In contrast, figures like Einstein and Schrödinger channel their survival instincts into exploring uncharted scientific realms. For them, survival extends beyond physical safety, venturing into intellectual legacy. Driven to solve the mysteries of the universe, they produced groundbreaking theories—relativity and quantum mechanics—spurred by a desire rooted in survival. Their quest to understand the world and contribute to human progress represents a profound form of intellectual survival.

This contrast in outcomes is striking. While both the crime boss and the scientist are motivated by survival, their intentions yield vastly different societal effects. The crime boss's approach may yield short-term gains but often sacrifices ethical standards and long-term stability. Conversely, the scientist's contributions have the potential to propel humanity forward, enhancing knowledge and quality of life. This demonstrates that, when positively directed, survival instincts can fuel transformative progress (Smith et al., 2023).

The implications are profound. Survival mechanisms are neither inherently moral nor immoral; they are adaptive. What matters is the direction these mechanisms take. Recognizing our shared survival drive fosters a better understanding of others' behaviors, whether they manifest constructively or destructively.

Additionally, societal myths play a vital role in structuring collaborative behavior. From ancient tales of gods and heroes to modern ideals of democracy and freedom, these narratives provide a framework within which survival instincts function, aligning individual actions with collaborative goals.

However, as societies evolve, so too must these narratives. We must cultivate stories that honor our shared survival imperatives while promoting equity, sustainability, and mutual respect. For example, fostering a narrative that celebrates scientific discovery and social cooperation as forms of survival can guide collaborative energies toward constructive outcomes (Waddock, 2023).

It is equally important to combine personal responsibility with social support for those facing hardship. Individuals should be encouraged to pursue survival goals ethically, while society should provide safety nets for those who encounter inevitable challenges. This fosters a resilient society where the primal drive for survival serves all, rather than dividing communities or inciting conflict.

When reflecting on the motivations behind diverse behaviors—whether it's the ambitions of a business tycoon or the innovations of a groundbreaking scientist—remember the common denominator: the survival imperative. This insight offers a pathway to developing policies and narratives that channel survival instincts toward the common good.

By understanding how deeply survival instincts are interwoven with human behavior, we can work towards a future where these impulses are tempered by wisdom and compassion, rather than fear and aggression. Achieving this balance is essential—for the sake of both individual fulfillment and societal harmony.

Activation of the Human Brain

In the realm of survival, the human brain acts as a master orchestrator, finely tuned to help us navigate threatening situations with maximum safety. When faced with danger, our brain initiates a complex interaction of neural circuits and hormonal releases. Imagine a life-threatening scenario: a dark alley at midnight, footsteps echoing behind you. In these moments, the amygdala ignites, activating the ancient fight-or-flight response.

This response is not merely theoretical; it is grounded in empirical evidence. Functional MRI studies show that regions associated with fear and decision-making activate intensely when we confront imminent danger, lighting up as if under a spotlight.

Interestingly, this response isn't limited to physical threats. Complex social scenarios can trigger similar neurological reactions. Take, for example, an intellectual debating on national television. Although not a life-or-death situation, the pressure and anxiety stimulate the same stress pathways. Research shows elevated activity in the prefrontal cortex— responsible for rational thinking—alongside the brain's more primal regions. This alignment suggests that our brain is wired to approach all challenges, from physical threats to high-stakes intellectual debates, with survival-oriented mechanisms (Shin and Liberzon, 2023).

The Brain's Response Across Diverse Contexts

Exploring further, the brain exhibits similar activation patterns in vastly different scenarios, such as crime and scientific discovery. For instance, a person planning a calculated crime engages multiple brain regions: the prefrontal cortex for planning, the limbic system for managing fear and excitement, and reward centers that anticipate the payoff. Though worlds apart, these actions share neurological similarities with the endeavors of scientists.

Imagine a scientist engrossed in solving a critical problem. Like the criminal, they engage in planning, feel the thrill of discovery, and anticipate rewards. Studies utilizing fMRI scans reveal that both criminal activity and scientific breakthroughs involve risk assessment, problem-solving, and the anticipation of reward. While differing in purpose, both scenarios reflect a pursuit of survival—navigating uncertainty and achieving success within their respective domains (Knutson and Huettel, 2021).

The Myth of a Higher Calling

Society often promotes the idea of a higher calling—driven by duty, curiosity, or altruism. While these motivations are valuable, they may sometimes obscure the brain's fundamental drive: survival. Even seemingly selfless acts can be traced back to evolutionary benefits. Take, for instance, a firefighter rushing into a burning building. Though motivated by duty, their brain processes risks, calculates paths, and actively works to ensure survival amidst fulfilling their role.

Evolution has crafted myths of higher purpose not only for individuals but for collaborative benefit. Societies thrive when individuals believe in causes greater than themselves. Such narratives foster order and cooperation, essential for communal survival. The key takeaway, however, remains clear: beneath these layers of ideology, the brain's primary trigger is survival (Mercier and Sperber, 2020). Understanding this doesn't diminish the value of high-minded aspirations; rather, it helps us appreciate the dual motives that drive human behavior. Recognizing the survival imperative allows for the design of societal structures and policies that resonate with these core instincts. In healthcare, for instance, understanding that fear of illness triggers similar survival mechanisms as actual illness can inform preventive care strategies. Likewise, in education, recognizing parallels between the stress of exams and real-world challenges can shape teaching methods that prepare students more effectively.

Implications for Policy-Making and Governance

With brains fundamentally wired for survival, policies that align with this intrinsic motivation are more likely to garner acceptance. Framing health and economic policies not merely as beneficial or moral obligations but as enhancements to collaborative and individual survival strengthens adherence.

Government and corporate collaboration, under transparent checks and balances, can foster environments where survival instincts are met with supportive structures rather than exploitative practices.

In essence, the brain's primary drive isn't inherently noble; it's grounded in ensuring survival. This understanding provides critical insights into shaping behaviors across society. Whether in criminals or intellectuals, survival mechanisms fundamentally influence actions.

Societal myths transform these impulses into structured motivations, benefiting both individuals and the collaborative. As these narratives evolve, integrating human welfare with economic growth, the path to sustainable progress becomes clearer and more resilient.

Societal Conditioning

Societies have long used stories to shape behavior, particularly to manage and channel primal survival instincts.

Humans have always been storytellers. From ancient cave paintings to modern films and novels, we create narratives that inform, entertain, and guide. These stories play an essential role in social conditioning, subtly instilling values, expectations, and behaviors deemed appropriate by society. Much of what we accept as societal norms has roots in fiction.

Myths and legends, for example, serve as moral compasses that influence generations, establishing codes of conduct and ideals that become embedded in culture. By shaping these stories, society pacifies and channels primal instincts, transforming raw survival imperatives into structured, cooperative behaviors. This narrative transformation provides a framework for individual actions aligned with collaborative goals, reinforcing social cohesion.

As we continue to adapt these stories, we can create narratives that champion survival in ways that promote cooperation, equity, and sustainability, steering collaborative behavior toward constructive outcomes.

Societal Conditioning Through Narrative

From early childhood, individuals are immersed in stories that teach lessons on right and wrong, heroism, loyalty, and the consequences of misconduct. Fairy tales, with their moral undertones, often depict good prevailing over evil, reinforcing societal expectations for ethical behavior. This early conditioning is not random; rather, it serves as a deliberate mechanism to prepare young minds for societal integration. Through these fables, children learn essential social survival skills—not for the wilderness, but for navigating social landscapes. They grasp how to function within a group, adhere to norms, and understand their roles (Fleer and Hammer, 2013).

In adolescence, narrative influences become particularly potent. As young people forge their identities and explore complex social dynamics, pop culture—movies, music, literature—plays a significant role. The stories portrayed in these media can inspire or discourage specific behaviors.

For example, rebellious characters may resonate with adolescents seeking independence, while cautionary tales of downfall can steer them away from risky actions. Modern superhero sagas, with their portrayals of valor and integrity, often serve as templates for youth, instilling ideals of justice, courage, and responsibility (Shackleford and Vinney, 2020).

The order maintained through these narratives is not solely aimed at pacifying the young; it stabilizes society as a whole. Growing up surrounded by consistent themes across various story forms, individuals internalize these messages, which in turn shape real-world actions and decisions. Society uses these stories to create a collaborative conscience—a shared understanding of what it means to belong to that society.

Stories as Anchors in Times of Crisis

In moments of crisis, stories serve as cultural and traditional control mechanisms. During upheavals, uncertainties, or even existential threats, societies rely on established narratives to avert chaos. These stories act as anchors, reminding people of past resilience, shared values, and hope for a better future.

Religious texts, historical accounts, and patriotic tales are invoked to inspire unity and perseverance. They provide both comfort and guidance, offering solace while instilling a sense of duty (Bietti, Tilston, and Bangerter, 2019).

Consider the use of myths during wartime. Leaders evoke legendary heroes and historic victories to rally troops and uplift civilian morale. These narratives are not merely grandiose tales; they are targeted psychological tools crafted to evoke purpose, belonging, and duty.

It's not just about surviving the immediate threat; it's about preserving the social fabric itself. The fundamental takeaway is that controlled narratives manage human survival instincts by embedding a framework of order and meaning.

By aligning individual behaviors with collaborative goals, societies ensure that the primal drive for survival reinforces, rather than disrupts, social harmony. This balance between personal freedom and social responsibility fosters an environment where economic growth and human welfare can coexist.

The Need for Evolving Narratives

For these narratives to remain effective, they must evolve to address modern challenges. Issues in healthcare, housing, education, and beyond demand stories that align with the complexities of contemporary life while managing basic instincts.

Today's narratives must champion collaborative efforts between governments and corporations that prioritize public welfare, reflecting a shift toward evidence-based policies that consider individual concerns (Crow and Jones, 2018).

The rise of science fiction and dystopian literature exemplifies this evolving narrative. These genres present futuristic scenarios that question our current paths and propose alternative visions.

Authors like George Orwell and Margaret Atwood not only tell compelling stories but also offer cautionary tales that provoke thought and inspire action. Dystopian narratives warn of potential pitfalls, yet they also encourage innovation and reform.

In conclusion, while controlled narratives have long served as the bedrock of societal stability, guiding behavior and reinforcing social norms, they must adapt to remain relevant.

By grounding these stories in empirical data and inclusivity, we ensure they continue to be effective tools for managing behavior in ways that balance economic growth with human welfare.

Evolution of Societal Narratives

Updating societal narratives does not mean discarding the foundational principles that have united communities for centuries. Rather, it involves fine-tuning these narratives to reflect contemporary realities while preserving core values. The goal is to balance the preservation of effective traditions with the integration of new insights, fostering a more inclusive and resilient society.

Societal programming establishes norms that guide human behavior, from survival instincts to intellectual aspirations. These cultural programs are as old as humanity, deeply embedded in collaborative experiences and myths passed down through generations. Just as our ancestors adapted to changes in their environments, our narratives must evolve to meet the challenges of modern life (Mesoudi, 2021).

Achieving Balance in Societal Narratives

To create a harmonious society that addresses contemporary needs while preserving core values, consider these approaches:

- Reflect on Timeless Values: Focus on values like fairness, cooperation, and respect—principles that have held societies together for centuries.

- Assess Compatibility with Modern Challenges: Evaluate how these values align with or clash against current societal norms, identifying areas that need adjustment.

- Encourage Public Discourse: Foster discussions on updating these values to meet present-day needs while preserving their essence.

- -Implement Adaptive Policies: Develop policies that support these updated narratives, ensuring they are flexible enough to evolve as society changes.

Learning from Ancient Wisdom

Our ancient ancestors intuitively understood their world, encoding survival strategies and moral lessons within myths and stories. By examining these ancient wisdoms, we can extract timeless lessons that resonate in today's context. Ancient societies, often facing existential threats, survived through adaptability and ingenuity. Their myths, though shrouded in symbolism and supernatural elements, conveyed messages of resilience, community unity, and moral guidance. For instance, many cultures have flood myths symbolizing rebirth after catastrophe—a powerful reminder as we face climate change and other large-scale disruptions.

Drawing Practical Applications from History

To translate ancient wisdom into actionable insights:

- Explore Historical Texts and Traditions: Dive into historical records and oral traditions to uncover lessons that have stood the test of time.

- Analyze Context: Understand the context in which these lessons emerged to grasp their broader significance.

- Modernize Lessons: Interpret these lessons in ways that address contemporary societal issues.

- Share through Education and Media: Disseminate these new interpretations to promote a broad understanding and acceptance.

Integrating ancient wisdom into modern life is not an exercise in nostalgia but a strategic approach to enrich the present. Ancient guidance on community living, resource management, and ethics offers invaluable perspectives on today's challenges in healthcare, housing, and education.

For example, indigenous practices emphasizing sustainable living and respect for nature are increasingly relevant in combating environmental degradation. Similarly, ancient philosophies that prioritized mental well-being and social harmony remind us that economic growth should not overshadow human welfare.

Strategies for Integrating Ancient Wisdom

- To incorporate these timeless principles into modern society:

- Identify Modern Parallels: Draw connections between ancient practices and current societal needs.

- Promote Interdisciplinary Research: Validate the relevance of these practices through collaboration across disciplines.

- Foster Cross-Sector Dialogues: Engage historians, scientists, policymakers, and community leaders in meaningful discussions.

- Create Accessible Platforms: Use books, podcasts, and forums to share and debate these insights with the public.

The Importance of Evolving Societal Narratives

As societies evolve, so too must the narratives that shape collaborative identity and behavior. Outdated narratives can lead to confusion and discord, making it essential for societal stories to progress alongside technological advancements, cultural shifts, and demographic changes. Consider the "American Dream," a story that once promised prosperity through hard work. While this narrative inspired generations, it has been criticized for overlooking systemic inequalities. Updating this story to reflect a more inclusive understanding of success—emphasizing social mobility, access to education, and equitable opportunities—can restore its unifying power.

Fostering Evolving Narratives

To ensure narratives remain relevant:

- Incorporate Diverse Perspectives: Involve a range of voices in creating and refining stories to reflect society's diversity.

- Critically Examine Existing Narratives**: Identify aspects that need revision to better serve today's society.

- Leverage Technology and Media**: Use digital platforms to widely and effectively disseminate updated stories.

- Commit to Continuous Revisions**: Regularly revisit and adapt narratives to align with societal advancements.

The human mind is deeply driven by the instinct to survive, which shapes behaviors across all walks of life. Whether in the actions of criminals or intellectuals, fundamental survival instincts underlie our choices, manifesting in diverse forms.

Societal myths and narratives are crucial for maintaining order and unity within communities. As we face unprecedented challenges, the need to update these narratives is more pressing than ever. By fine-tuning our societal programming, drawing from the wisdom of our ancestors, and integrating these insights into our modern context, we can navigate new challenges while preserving essential societal structures.

Evolving our collaborative stories is not simply a task; it is an imperative for sustaining human progress and fostering a compassionate, resilient society.

Through thoughtful reflection and strategic adaptation, we can shape narratives that support both individual fulfillment and collaborative well-being—stories that inspire, unify, and drive meaningful progress for generations to come.

Sustaining Progress Through Evolved Narratives

In this chapter, we have explored the fundamental force driving human behavior—the survival imperative. This examination has traversed different layers of society, revealing how primal instincts surface in both criminals and intellectuals. We have also highlighted the crucial role that societal myths play in fostering order and coherence within communities.

As previously discussed, the human brain is at its most resourceful when navigating survival pressures. Whether it's a crime boss strategizing to maintain power or a scientist probing the secrets of the universe, the end goal remains similar: to secure one's existence and build a legacy. This core drive is the foundation of actions that can be either constructive or destructive, depending on the path taken.

Reflecting on the impact of our survival instincts, we must recognize their dual nature. While these drives can lead to remarkable achievements, they also harbor the potential to incite conflict and destabilize society if not channeled constructively. Acknowledging this balance calls for reflection on how individual behaviors influence the collaborative well-being of society.

On a broader scale, understanding the depth of our survival mechanisms provides valuable insights for designing effective policies and shaping societal narratives. Aligning personal ambitions with the common good builds a society that fosters both individual fulfillment and communal stability. Neglecting this balance risks intensifying social divides and conflicts, ultimately hindering sustainable progress.

This brings us to the evident need for evolving societal stories. Our myths and narratives must adapt to meet contemporary challenges while retaining the wisdom embedded within them. This evolution ensures that our survival instincts are steered by empathy and foresight, rather than by fear and hostility.

As we continue to navigate the complexities of modern life, we must aspire to craft new narratives that champion equity, sustainability, and mutual respect. This ongoing evolution is more than a task; it is a necessity for sustaining human progress and achieving a harmonious future. By continually refining our collaborative stories, we can inspire a society that not only survives but also thrives, paving the way for a resilient and compassionate world.

Chapter 2
The Role of Storytelling in Human Behavior

Stories have always served as more than mere entertainment; they are essential components of human culture and expression. From the tales shared around ancient campfires to the narratives found in today's blockbuster films, storytelling has consistently acted as a means of sharing wisdom and values across generations.

This chapter will explore how stories have not only reflected societal norms but have actively shaped human behavior throughout history. By examining techniques used by ancient storytellers and the impact of contemporary narratives, we can gain a deeper appreciation for storytelling's enduring influence on collaborative consciousness.

Ancient narratives, such as the "Epic of Gilgamesh" and Greek myths, were intricately crafted with symbolic meanings, serving as moral and ethical guides for listeners. For example, the "Mahabharata" in Indian culture encapsulates a vast array of human experiences and philosophical challenges, providing a narrative framework to understand complex concepts like duty and righteousness.

These stories were not merely passed down orally but were integrated into rituals, festivals, and public performances, making them an essential part of communal life. As societies evolved and technology advanced, storytelling mediums shifted from oral traditions to written texts, which further preserved these tales and added layers of depth to their meanings.

In the following pages, this chapter will delve into the crafting and transmission of ancient stories, focusing on the use of allegories and metaphors to convey profound truths. It will also examine the creation of modern narratives that address contemporary societal needs while drawing inspiration from ancient wisdom.

Additionally, the chapter will explore the future of storytelling, considering the roles of technology and artificial intelligence in shaping new forms of narratives. By understanding this evolution, readers can appreciate how stories bridge generational gaps and continue to shape societal norms and behaviors (Lugmayr et al., 2022).

Historical Perspective on Stories

Ancient stories were much more than entertainment; they formed the foundation upon which societies constructed norms and values. These narratives, intricately woven with layered meanings, have served as moral guides and societal blueprints, influencing human behavior across generations.

For example, the "Epic of Gilgamesh," one of the world's oldest known literary works, explores themes like friendship, mortality, and the quest for purpose—issues that remain relevant today. Examining such ancient stories reveals how they helped mold the ethos of entire communities, providing frameworks for navigating life's complexities.

In Ancient Greece, myths transcended mere tales and served as educational tools. Stories of gods, heroes, and mythical beings conveyed lessons on courage, honor, and justice. Shared in public spaces like the agora, these narratives instilled a collaborative consciousness among citizens, reinforcing communal values while celebrating individual heroism—a balance that resonates in modern societies as well.

Similarly, the Indian epic "Mahabharata" encompasses a wide range of human experiences and ethical challenges, highlighting the importance of duty (dharma) and the consequences of abandoning it. Characters such as Yudhishthira and Arjuna personify righteousness and moral struggle, respectively. These stories provided a narrative framework for complex philosophical concepts, making them accessible and relatable (Zajko and Hoyle, 2022).

Understanding how these stories were crafted and transmitted is crucial. Storytelling in ancient times was primarily an oral tradition, with tales passed down through generations by word of mouth. Storytellers, known as griots in some cultures, held revered positions and were entrusted with preserving history and wisdom. The cadence, rhythm, and repetition characteristic of oral storytelling were not random; they were deliberate techniques designed to aid memory and ensure accuracy.

The dissemination of these stories extended beyond verbal recounting; they were also embedded in rituals and ceremonies. Festivals, dances, and theatrical performances often centered around these narratives, weaving them into the fabric of daily life. For instance, Greek tragedies performed during the festival of Dionysia were not solely for entertainment; they were communal reflections on human nature and societal values.

The Future of Storytelling

As technology and artificial intelligence continue to reshape how we create and consume stories, the core principles of storytelling remain. Future narratives will likely retain elements of timeless themes while adapting to new mediums and perspectives. By examining storytelling's evolution, from oral traditions to digital media, we can see how narratives continue to shape individual identities and social values across generations.

Storytelling's role in human behavior extends beyond cultural transmission; it is a powerful tool that shapes societal values and individual behaviors. By studying both ancient and modern narratives, we gain insights into how stories provide a cohesive framework for collaborative identity, moral guidance, and societal resilience. As we move forward, it is essential to preserve the wisdom of traditional storytelling while adapting it to address contemporary challenges and needs. Through this ongoing evolution, storytelling remains a vital force in guiding human behavior and shaping the future of society.

As societies evolved and writing systems developed, stories found new media, transitioning from oral traditions to written forms. This shift not only preserved these tales but also introduced additional layers of complexity and nuance. Manuscripts became treasured artifacts, meticulously copied by hand to ensure the endurance of cultural heritage across generations.

Allegories and metaphors are central to many ancient stories, serving as powerful tools for conveying deeper truths. Aesop's Fables, for instance, though simple on the surface, use animals and inanimate objects to impart wisdom about human behavior. The story of "The Tortoise and the Hare" extends beyond its literal narrative, teaching lessons on perseverance and humility (Zipes, 2021).

Similarly, biblical parables like "The Good Samaritan" provide profound moral and ethical guidance by presenting scenarios that encourage self-reflection. These metaphorical tales enable people to grasp complex concepts intuitively, making intricate ideas accessible and impactful.

The influence of these ancient narratives persists in contemporary storytelling. Modern writers and filmmakers frequently draw inspiration from age-old motifs, reinterpreting them for present-day audiences while preserving their core messages. The timeless nature of these stories lies in their ability to address fundamental human concerns—love, loss, ambition, betrayal, and redemption.

For instance, the "Harry Potter" series resonates deeply with readers by tapping into archetypal themes from ancient myths, such as the hero's journey, the struggle between good and evil, and the quest for identity.

J.K. Rowling's saga serves as a modern allegory that speaks to readers' values of justice, bravery, and friendship (Grimes, 2022).

Creating contemporary narratives that resonate with current societal needs while drawing on ancient wisdom is crucial for bridging generational divides. Storytelling becomes a conduit for shared experiences and understanding, fostering a sense of continuity and belonging. In our rapidly changing world, these stories act as anchor points, reminding us of enduring values amid uncertainty.

Looking ahead, the future of storytelling promises further evolution, especially with the rise of technology and artificial intelligence. Digital storytelling platforms and virtual reality experiences are reshaping how stories are told and consumed, offering immersive, interactive experiences that allow users to participate actively in the narrative rather than merely observing.

Artificial intelligence also holds potential in shaping future narratives. Algorithms can analyze vast amounts of data to generate personalized stories, catering to individual preferences and creating unique, engaging experiences. However, this technological shift raises questions about authorship and authenticity. While AI can replicate the structure and style of traditional storytelling, it lacks the depth of emotion and lived experience that human storytellers contribute (Sloan, 2020).

Yet, despite these innovations, the essence of storytelling remains unchanged. At its core, storytelling is about connection, shared experiences, and finding meaning in the world. Whether through ancient epics or cutting-edge virtual realities, stories transcend time and space, touching hearts and minds across generations.

In conclusion, ancient stories serve as a timeless blueprint for societal norms and values, providing insights that continue to resonate in the present. By examining the craftsmanship and transmission of these narratives, appreciating their allegorical and metaphorical depth, and recognizing the interplay between past wisdom and future innovation, we can harness the enduring power of storytelling to build a more connected and compassionate society. As we navigate the complexities of modern life, these age-old tales offer guidance and inspiration, illuminating our path forward in an increasingly intricate world.

Creating Modern Narratives

To craft contemporary stories that resonate deeply with today's societal needs, we must first recognize the importance of developing new vocabulary, metaphors, and allegories. Just as ancient cultures devised terms and tales to interpret their world, our era demands a similar evolution in storytelling, particularly around concepts like Artificial Intelligence (AI). The way we frame AI today will profoundly influence its integration into society.

Consider AI as an entirely new "species"—engineered by humans yet capable of evolving and interacting in ways that mirror human behaviors. Effectively communicating this concept requires a language that captures the nuance and complexity of these interactions. We need fresh metaphors and allegories to create vivid portrayals of AI's role, potential, and ethical implications. By likening AI to mythological figures or drawing from nature, we can help people intuitively grasp its capabilities and boundaries.

Here are essential steps to achieve this goal:

- **Study existing scientific literature and philosophical works on** AI to build a comprehensive understanding.

- **Collaborate with linguists and storytellers** to brainstorm and coin new terms that vividly describe AI's characteristics.

- **Develop rich allegories and metaphors** that capture the essence of AI-human interaction, drawing from both modern and ancient cultural references.

- **Test these narratives through various media** to gauge public reaction, refining them for clarity and impact.

By iterating on these stories, we cultivate a common understanding of AI's place in our lives, equipping society to navigate this complex terrain with informed perspectives.

The evolution of language is vital to this process. Language is not static; it adapts to societal shifts, technological progress, and cultural exchange. This transformation allows us to articulate new ideas and adapt to change. As we introduce novel concepts—such as AI as a near-sentient entity—language must evolve to encapsulate these notions accurately.

Modern storytelling should reflect this dynamism. As we craft narratives today, we should embrace linguistic innovation. Words and phrases that might seem unconventional now could become standards in the future. Consider how terms like "selfie" or "tweet" integrated seamlessly into our lexicon due to technological advances. Similarly, terms like "machine learning," "neural networks," and "deep fakes" have emerged, marking our growing familiarity with AI (Mufwene, 2021).

Effective communication about AI and other emerging technologies depends on our ability to coin terms that are both precise and accessible. This ensures broader engagement and understanding, fostering informed discourse rather than fear or misunderstanding.

The impact of modern stories on societal behavior is profound. Stories are not mere entertainment; they influence our values, beliefs, and actions. Narratives about AI shape public perception and policymaking, affecting how governments regulate technology, how businesses implement AI solutions, and how individuals interact with intelligent systems in daily life.

When we ground modern narratives in ancient wisdom while addressing current societal needs, we bridge generational gaps. Ancient stories carry timeless insights into human nature, ethics, and the cosmos. By weaving these elements into contemporary narratives, we connect past and present, demonstrating that while tools and contexts may change, core human concerns remain constant (Bilandzic and Busselle, 2021).

For example, the myth of Prometheus, who brought fire to humanity, can be reimagined to represent the dawn of AI, portraying it as a powerful tool with immense potential and significant risks. Through such narratives, we underscore the need for responsible innovation and caution against hubris.

As technology evolves, so will our narratives. The future of storytelling will be shaped by advancements in areas like virtual reality, augmented reality, and AI itself. Imagine a world where stories are not only read or watched but experienced firsthand through immersive technologies. This shift could revolutionize how we communicate complex concepts and emotions, making storytelling more interactive and impactful.

AI itself can play a transformative role in this evolution. AI-driven algorithms can analyze vast datasets to identify emerging trends, ensuring stories remain relevant and resonant. These systems can also personalize narratives, tailoring them to individual preferences and enhancing engagement and emotional connection.

However, as we embrace these technologies, balance is essential. While AI can assist in crafting and delivering stories, human creativity and intuition must remain at the core. Stories, at their heart, are about human experience, and the human touch is irreplaceable. Technology should enhance rather than diminish the authenticity of our narratives (Riedl, 2021).

In conclusion, crafting contemporary stories requires a careful blend of innovation and tradition. Creating new vocabulary, metaphors, and allegories for AI and other modern phenomena is critical for effective communication. Language must keep pace with societal changes, ensuring that we can convey new ideas clearly and compellingly.

Modern narratives have a powerful influence on societal behavior, shaping values and guiding actions. By anchoring these stories in ancient wisdom and addressing current needs, we bridge generational divides, fostering a deeper understanding of our world.

As we look toward the future, technology will play an essential role in storytelling. Yet, amid these advancements, the essence of storytelling—the human touch—must remain central. By striking this balance, we can create narratives that not only entertain but also enlighten and inspire, guiding society toward a more informed and compassionate future.

Bridging Generations with Stories

Let's embark on our journey to understand how stories bridge generational gaps. Each generation brings unique experiences and contexts that shape its worldview. Baby Boomers, for example, grew up in a post-war era where radio and television were primary information sources. In contrast, Millennials and Gen Z are digital natives, with the internet ever-present in their lives.

Yet, despite these differences, stories remain a timeless medium of communication. They create a shared space where diverse experiences can intersect. Effective storytelling involves crafting narratives that resonate across generational divides by incorporating values and norms relevant to each generation's cultural backdrop. For instance, a story centered on perseverance might emphasize community spirit to appeal to older audiences, while highlighting innovation and adaptability to engage younger listeners.

Here are actionable steps to foster intergenerational connection through storytelling:

- **Listen to cherished stories from different generations** within your audience. These stories form a foundation that, when interwoven with contemporary elements, creates relatability.

- **Blend these traditional narratives with modern elements,** ensuring they resonate with today's world.

- **Incorporate universal themes**—such as love, loss, triumph, and failure—so that the story's core message remains accessible to all ages.

- **Use modern media to present ancient wisdom through** visual aids, social media snippets, and interactive applications, bridging generational divides.

Turning to the role of parents and educators, these storytellers have historically been the guardians of cultural knowledge, passing down lessons through parables, fables, and myths. Their role transcends simply preserving old tales; it involves adapting and contextualizing them to instill values that resonate across time.

Parents and educators should intentionally select stories that promote empathy, curiosity, and critical thinking. By fostering an environment where young minds are encouraged to question and discuss, we ensure that these stories evolve with each retelling, enriched by fresh perspectives. Their influence is profound; they lay the foundation for a lifelong appreciation of narrative as a means to understand the world (Cremin et al., 2018).

Guiding principles for effective storytelling in educational settings include:

- **Encouraging active participation** from listeners, allowing them to engage with the story by reflecting and discussing.

- **Utilizing storytelling techniques** that involve vivid descriptions, emotional engagement, and moral dilemmas that provoke thought.

- **Incorporating multimedia resources** like films, audiobooks, and interactive apps to cater to diverse learning preferences.

- **Regularly updating stories to reflect current societal challenges,** blending historical lessons with contemporary issues.

Adapting stories for contemporary relevance is essential. Modern society's unique challenges and opportunities require reframing ancient wisdom to maintain its resonance. This involves interpreting traditional narratives through the lens of present-day realities.

Take the Greek myth of Icarus as an example. Traditionally, it warns against hubris and excessive ambition. Today, it could be reframed to discuss balancing ambition with mental health or exploring the consequences of ignoring climate change warnings. By drawing parallels between ancient lessons and current events, we create a tapestry where the past informs the present and guides future actions (Zajko and Hoyle, 2021).

Steps for incorporating contemporary relevance into ancient stories include:

- **Identifying the core message of the original story** and relating it to modern societal issues.

- **Reframing characters and settings** to reflect present-day contexts, making the story more relatable.

- **Using technology to enhance the storytelling experience,** such as augmented reality (AR) or virtual reality (VR) for immersive engagement.

- **Drawing connections between ancient stories and recent events,** helping listeners appreciate the enduring applicability of these lessons.

The key takeaway here is that effective storytelling connects generations and conveys enduring values. Whether conveyed through oral traditions, written texts, or digital platforms, stories serve as vessels carrying cultural wisdom across time. When thoughtfully woven, stories entertain, educate, inspire, and unite, helping us understand our identity and heritage while offering insight into our future path.

Storytelling has tremendous potential to bridge generational divides. Through stories, we share our collaborative history and identity, nurturing unity amidst diversity. As we navigate modern complexities, returning to storytelling can provide the context and continuity needed for cohesive societal evolution (Lugmayr et al., 2023).

In conclusion, whether you are a parent sharing a bedtime story, an educator incorporating stories into your curriculum, or a writer drawing from ancient wisdom, remember that the stories you tell today shape the narratives of tomorrow. Stories are the threads that weave the fabric of our shared humanity, and through them, we can strengthen bonds across generations, guiding us toward a more connected and understanding world.

The Future of Storytelling

The impact of technology on storytelling has been transformative, reshaping the ways stories are created, shared, and consumed. From the invention of the printing press to the rise of digital media, each technological leap has unlocked new avenues for narrative expression. Today, in our hyper-connected world, stories can reach global audiences in seconds—a feat that would have been unimaginable in the past.

Consider the role of social media platforms. These platforms have revolutionized storytelling by democratizing content creation, allowing storytelling to extend beyond traditional gatekeepers like publishing houses or film studios. Now, anyone with internet access and a device can share their narrative, empowering individuals to express their experiences and perspectives and enriching the collaborative tapestry of human stories.

Yet, this democratization brings complexities. While social media enables wide dissemination, it also creates an environment where misinformation can proliferate. To navigate this double-edged sword, cultivating critical thinking skills and an awareness of technology's influence on the stories we consume is essential. Only through this discernment can we fully harness the positive potential of this technological expansion (Lund, Cohen, and Scarles, 2018).

The rise of artificial intelligence marks the frontier of yet another transformative era in storytelling. AI algorithms capable of processing vast amounts of data are now used to generate immersive narratives. For example, companies like OpenAI have developed language models that can produce coherent and compelling text, blurring the boundaries between human and machine-generated content.

This technological advancement opens exciting possibilities. AI could support writers by outlining plots, developing characters, or drafting scenes, making the creative process more accessible. Additionally, AI might allow for personalized storytelling experiences where narratives adapt based on an individual's preferences and responses. The potential for innovation is immense.

However, these advancements come with ethical considerations. If AI-generated stories become indistinguishable from human-created ones, what does this mean for authenticity? How can we ensure that such technologies are used responsibly, without diminishing the value of human creativity? These questions demand thoughtful consideration as we venture further into this uncharted territory (Rettberg, 2019).

As technology and AI reshape storytelling mechanisms, challenges in maintaining cultural coherence will likely emerge. Stories have long been fundamental to cultural identity, conveying values, traditions, and norms across generations. With the rapid pace of technological change, the risk of losing this coherence becomes more pronounced.

For instance, the vast array of online content brings both enrichment and fragmentation to cultural discourse. While diverse storytelling broadens our cultural fabric, it can also encourage individuals to retreat into niche communities and echo chambers, potentially weakening shared identity. The challenge, then, is fostering an environment where diverse narratives coexist while contributing to a cohesive cultural dialogue.

Furthermore, as AI takes on a greater role in narrative production, it is crucial to consider which voices are amplified and which may be sidelined. Efforts must be made to ensure inclusivity so that the richness of human experience is preserved and celebrated rather than obscured.

Looking forward, the evolution of storytelling will continue to be shaped by technology, influencing future societal norms. The stories we tell—and how we tell them—encapsulate our collaborative aspirations, fears, and dreams. As technological advancements create new pathways for narrative expression, they will also redefine the societal contexts within which these stories unfold.

The potential integration of augmented reality (AR) and virtual reality (VR) in storytelling is particularly compelling. Imagine a world where stories are not simply read or watched but fully experienced through immersive environments. These technologies could create powerful empathetic bridges, allowing individuals to experience others' perspectives in ways that words alone cannot achieve (Murray, 2018).

However, amidst these innovations, it is vital to stay grounded in our humanity. Storytelling, at its essence, is a profoundly human endeavor, rooted in sharing insights, building connections, and fostering understanding. As we embrace new tools and methods, we must strive to preserve the core of what makes a story resonate: its capacity to touch the human spirit.

To sum up, storytelling will continue to evolve alongside technology, fundamentally shaping future societal norms. The challenge and opportunity lie in using these advancements to enhance human welfare, ensuring that even in an age dominated by screens and algorithms, the heart of storytelling—the forging of human connection—remains vibrant and enduring (Lugmayr et al., 2022).

As we navigate this evolving landscape, we should honor the timeless wisdom in ancient narratives while embracing the innovative forces propelling contemporary storytelling. In doing so, we bridge generational divides, creating a continuum that respects the past, engages the present, and looks toward the future with hope and curiosity. The future of storytelling holds immense promise. As we stand on the brink of this new horizon, let us approach it with a balanced reverence for tradition and enthusiasm for innovation, ensuring that the age-old practice of storytelling adapts to reflect and shape our ever-changing world.

The Ever-Evolving Tale of Human Society

In this chapter, we have explored the intricate interplay between storytelling and human behavior, tracing how ancient narratives have shaped societal evolution through their creation, transmission, and enduring impact. From the "Epic of Gilgamesh" to Greek myths and Indian epics, we examined the significance of these stories as moral compasses and cultural frameworks that continue to influence us.

Looking back, it becomes clear that storytelling has always been more than mere entertainment. It is a powerful vehicle for instilling values and providing frameworks to navigate life's complexities. This tradition of passing down wisdom through stories has evolved from oral recounting to written manuscripts and now to digital media, embedding stories within rituals, ceremonies, and diverse modern platforms.

In examining the transition from ancient to contemporary narratives, we recognized the importance of crafting stories that resonate with current societal needs while drawing on ancient wisdom. Storytelling, therefore, becomes a bridge across generations, fostering a sense of continuity and belonging in a rapidly changing world.

Looking to the future, the influence of technology and artificial intelligence promises to reshape storytelling in unprecedented ways. Digital platforms, virtual reality, and AI are transforming how stories are created, shared, and experienced, offering immersive, interactive ways to engage with narratives. AI has the potential to generate personalized stories, but it also raises questions around authenticity and the irreplaceable value of human creativity (Lugmayr et al., 2023).

These advancements present exciting opportunities but demand careful consideration. The ethical implications of AI-driven narratives, the preservation of cultural coherence amid technological shifts, and the balance between innovation and tradition are challenges we must thoughtfully navigate. Despite evolving mediums, the essence of storytelling—connecting with others and finding meaning—remains unchanged.

Ultimately, storytelling continues to be a powerful bridge across generations, preserving timeless truths and guiding us toward deeper understanding of ourselves and the world. Drawing inspiration from ancient narratives and embracing new technologies, we can craft stories that not only entertain but also enlighten and unite, shaping a more connected and compassionate society. Moving forward, let us honor the past while innovatively crafting the future, ensuring that the threads of our shared humanity remain vibrant and resilient.

Chapter 3

The Evolution of Human Societies and the Awareness of Human Boundaries

The story of human societies is a tapestry woven from threads of cooperation, innovation, and the drive to thrive in an ever-changing world. From the simplicity of early hunter-gatherer communities to the complexity of modern civilizations, our journey has been defined by profound transformations in the ways we live, communicate, and organize. This evolution is not merely a chronicle of technological advancements or economic growth; it is a testament to our collaborative ability to observe, adapt, and transcend boundaries—both physical and conceptual.

A defining aspect of this journey has been societies' growing understanding of, and respect for, various boundaries. Early humans navigated their environments with caution, observing territorial limits set by other groups to avoid conflict and ensure survival. As societies expanded and became more intricate, these boundaries grew to encompass not only physical spaces but also cultural, cognitive, psychological, and spiritual dimensions. For instance, the development of language and writing allowed us to document observations and share knowledge, laying the groundwork for organized social structures. Likewise, cultural norms and social etiquettes evolved to maintain harmony within increasingly dense populations. Failing to respect these boundaries often led to social unrest, diminished trust, and, in some cases, the collapse of entire civilizations (Mauser et al., 2020).

In this chapter, we will examine the nuanced development of human societies through the lens of boundary awareness. We will trace the progression from simple hunter-gatherer bands to the emergence of complex civilizations, underscoring the impact of documentation and communication tools in shaping societal structures.

Next, we will explore the importance of understanding and maintaining different types of boundaries—physical, cognitive, psychological, and spiritual—and how these boundaries have been essential for fostering both social cohesion and individual well-being. By studying the forces that compelled our ancestors to evolve and adapt, we gain valuable insights into the delicate balance necessary to sustain thriving human communities today and in the future.

Physical Boundaries

Recognizing and respecting physical boundaries is essential to fostering healthy and constructive human interactions. Acknowledging others' personal space goes beyond social courtesy—it establishes an environment of mutual respect and trust. Human societies, from early formations to today's complex civilizations, have always been guided by implicit and explicit norms that govern interactions within shared spaces. Physical boundaries form a core part of these norms.

Respecting someone's physical boundary involves understanding their need for personal space, which varies according to cultural background, individual preferences, and situational contexts. Empathy and attentiveness are key to this respect, enhancing our social bonds. Consider a crowded subway: even in such confined quarters, people instinctively adjust their posture to minimize unnecessary contact, subtly negotiating their physical boundaries to maintain comfort despite close proximity (Kreuz & Roberts, 2019).

Here are practical steps for recognizing and respecting physical boundaries:

- **Observe non-verbal** cues such as body language. Signs like stepping back, crossing arms, or averting gaze may indicate discomfort with closeness.

- **Seek permission before initiating physical contact**, whether it's a handshake, hug, or even a tap on the shoulder.

- **Respect others' verbalized preferences** about personal space. If someone expresses a need for more space or discomfort with physical touch, honor their request without questioning or expecting justification.

Violating physical boundaries can have profound impacts. When a person's boundaries are ignored, it can lead to discomfort, anxiety, or even trauma, eroding trust and undermining relationships. For instance, in the workplace, where professional decorum often dictates a respectful distance, encroaching on someone's space can be perceived as invasive or aggressive, potentially leading to conflicts or disciplinary actions.

In more severe cases, disregarding physical boundaries can result in legal repercussions, particularly in instances of harassment or assault. This highlights the importance of educating individuals about physical boundaries from a young age, fostering respect for others' personal space as a foundation for safe and supportive communities (Aboujaoude et al., 2022).

Maintaining and Communicating Physical Boundaries

To uphold both your own boundaries and respect others', clear communication is essential. Articulating personal boundaries explicitly and assertively can help prevent discomfort. Simple phrases like "I need a bit more personal space" or "I'm not comfortable with hugs" allow you to express your needs without ambiguity.

Consistency in maintaining boundaries also plays a vital role. When you consistently set and uphold your boundaries, others will recognize and respect them over time. For example, if you prefer a certain distance during conversations, gently stepping back whenever someone gets too close can help establish this as a standard.

Creating and maintaining boundaries also involves self-awareness. Regularly checking in with yourself to assess your comfort levels in different situations enables you to adjust your boundaries proactively. It's crucial to remember that boundaries are not static; they can shift based on context and relationship dynamics. Allow yourself the flexibility to modify them as needed (Pratscher et al., 2019).

For instance, while you may feel comfortable with a close friend standing nearby during a conversation, you may need more space with a colleague or stranger. Recognizing these variations and adjusting accordingly ensures that your boundaries remain relevant and effective.

Lastly, promote awareness of physical boundaries by sharing your knowledge and experiences. Encourage open discussions about personal space and respect among friends, family, and colleagues to foster an environment where everyone feels comfortable expressing their needs and listening to others' preferences.

By integrating these practices into our daily lives, we contribute to a culture that values and respects physical boundaries, establishing a foundation for healthier, more harmonious interactions. This, in turn, enhances individual well-being and collaborative societal health.

As we trace human society's evolution from hunter-gatherer communities to modern civilizations, it becomes evident that successful social development depends on our capacity to negotiate and respect one another's physical and emotional spaces (Alaimo and Tong, 2020).

In Conclusion, respecting physical boundaries transcends social convention; it acknowledges the intrinsic value of each person's personal space and cultivates an atmosphere of safety and respect. Moving from mere recognition of these boundaries to actively implementing strategies for their maintenance in our daily lives can significantly strengthen our relationships. Let us strive to balance economic growth with human welfare, prioritize empathy in our interactions, and advocate for policies and practices that honor the sanctity of personal space.

Cognitive Boundaries

Understanding cognitive boundaries may initially seem abstract, yet it centers on recognizing the limits of our mental capabilities and maintaining clear mental space. Cognitive boundaries function like invisible fences around our minds, safeguarding our thoughts, emotions, and energy from undue interference or overload. Picture them as unseen barriers that preserve our mental clarity and focus, allowing us to process information effectively and make well-informed decisions.

Consider our daily reality: we're continually bombarded by information—social media notifications, work emails, personal interactions, and myriad opinions. Without strong cognitive boundaries, it becomes all too easy to feel overwhelmed, leading to heightened stress and reduced productivity. Understanding these boundaries is crucial for anyone seeking to maintain mental health and efficiency (Firth et al., 2019).

A common example of a cognitive boundary violation is multitasking in focus-oriented environments, such as trying to engage in a meaningful conversation while also checking emails or scrolling through social media. Another frequent violation occurs when we allow others to intrude excessively into our thinking space. This may happen when colleagues flood us with non-urgent concerns during critical working hours or when friends habitually unload their issues without considering our emotional bandwidth. Such scenarios disrupt cognitive equilibrium, impairing our ability to concentrate on tasks that require deep thought and creativity.

Protecting cognitive space involves practical strategies to reduce mental clutter and enhance focus. To maintain cognitive boundaries effectively:

- **Prioritize tasks and set dedicated times for different activities.** Schedule 'focus time' free from distractions to enable deeper engagement with critical tasks.

- **Practice mindfulness and self-awareness.** Regular check-ins help detect signs of cognitive overload. Techniques like deep breathing and meditation can restore mental clarity.

- **Develop assertive communication.** Politely but firmly set limits on interruptions that encroach on your mental space. For instance, if a colleague approaches you with non-urgent matters during focus time, let them know you'll address their concern after completing your task.

By implementing these practices, you create a protective buffer around your mental processes, helping to maintain focus and reduce stress. Cognitive boundaries are not about isolating oneself but fostering selective openness to function optimally, both personally and socially. To understand the importance of cognitive boundaries, consider the evolution of human societies from hunter-gatherer bands to complex civilizations. Our ancestors, though spared the constant data influx we experience today, had to navigate their cognitive landscapes with discernment to survive. They developed tools, language, and social cooperation—achievements that required focused cognitive effort.

As societies advanced, cognitive boundaries became essential. The invention of written language enabled knowledge documentation, sparking breakthroughs in science and technology.

However, the complexity of social structures introduced new challenges. Maintaining cohesive and effective organizations required clear distinctions between roles and responsibilities, essentially establishing cognitive boundaries at a communal level (Nagels et al., 2013).

Today, cognitive boundaries play a role beyond individual mental health; they are vital to collaborative behavior and societal well-being. With technological advancements blurring the line between work and personal life, maintaining cognitive boundaries is essential in preventing burnout and promoting sustainable productivity.

The concept of cognitive boundaries also applies to broader societal contexts. In policy-making, for example, decision-makers must distinguish between empirical evidence and subjective opinion to ensure policies are guided by reliable data. This reduces cognitive overload and enhances governance quality.

The key takeaway is simple yet powerful: cognitive boundaries help maintain mental clarity and focus. By recognizing their importance and actively protecting cognitive space, we can navigate the complexities of modern life with greater ease and efficiency.

We owe it to ourselves—and to future generations—to understand and respect these boundaries, fostering a balanced approach to personal growth and societal progress (Sonnentag and Bayer, 2022).

As you move forward, whether in personal pursuits or professional settings, remember to guard your cognitive space diligently. Protecting mental clarity is not merely a strategy for success but a foundation for a fulfilled and purposeful life. By honoring these boundaries, we enable ourselves and our society to flourish, achieving a harmonious balance between economic progress and human welfare.

Psychological Boundaries

The concept of psychological boundaries plays a pivotal role in understanding human societal evolution. Psychological boundaries are the invisible barriers that define and protect our emotional and mental space.

These boundaries are critical in shaping how we interact with others and the world around us. By setting limits on what we are willing to accept, psychological boundaries help safeguard our emotional health and well-being. Historically, psychological boundaries have influenced social interactions within communities. In hunter-gatherer societies, close-knit groups depended on mutual respect and an understanding of individual space and roles. Recognizing and honoring these boundaries was essential for group cohesion and survival. As societies developed, these tacit understandings were woven into cultural norms and practices, influencing everything from family dynamics to broader social hierarchies (Dunbar, 2022).

However, breaches of psychological boundaries can significantly impact emotional stability. When someone violates our mental or emotional space—whether through disrespect, manipulation, or privacy intrusions—it can lead to feelings of anxiety, stress, or even depression. Such boundary violations are not solely individual issues; they affect society as well. Just as breaches of physical boundaries can provoke conflict, so can breaches of psychological boundaries strain relationships and disrupt community harmony.

Technological advances and changing social structures have further complicated these dynamics. Social media, for example, blurs the lines of personal space, often leading to increased scrutiny and judgment. This shift necessitates greater awareness and mindfulness regarding our interactions, both online and face-to-face. Safeguarding our psychological well-being requires intentionality and proactive measures.

Here are practical ways to maintain healthy psychological boundaries:

- **Understand your limits:** Recognize what makes you uncomfortable or stressed. Self-awareness is essential for setting clear boundaries.

- **Communicate assertively:** Clearly express your needs and expectations. Let others know and respect your limits.

- **Practice self-care:** Regularly engage in activities that nurture mental and emotional health, whether through hobbies, exercise, meditation, or quiet time.

- **Establish digital boundaries:** Be mindful of your online presence and interactions. Limit exposure to intrusive content, and curate a supportive social media experience.

- **Seek support when needed:** Reach out to friends, family, or professionals if you struggle to maintain boundaries.

Implementing these strategies fosters healthier relationships with oneself and others, enhancing overall societal well-being.

Interestingly, these principles echo through history. Ancient civilizations developed complex etiquette and social norms that acted as psychological boundaries, managing interactions within increasingly intricate societies. For example, in many indigenous cultures, rituals and ceremonies governed access to sacred spaces and knowledge, fostering respect for both personal and collaborative boundaries.

In our interconnected world, the need to maintain psychological boundaries has become even more apparent. The digital age offers immense opportunities for growth and collaboration, but it also challenges us to preserve personal space amidst constant connectivity.

Balancing these aspects requires conscious effort and collaborative understanding (Vorderer and Kohring, 2023).

Governments and corporations play a role in this dynamic. Policies that promote mental health awareness, encourage workplace respect, and protect individual privacy support societal efforts to maintain healthy boundaries.

Corporations, in particular, must recognize their influence on social norms and prioritize the well-being of employees and consumers. Collaboration between public and private sectors, with proper checks and balances, can create environments conducive to respecting psychological boundaries (Government of Canada, 2019).

Ultimately, empowerment rests with individuals. Education and advocacy are key to this endeavor. By raising awareness of psychological boundaries and providing tools for mental health protection, we can foster more resilient communities. Schools, workplaces, and community organizations can contribute to this mission by incorporating mental health education and promoting open dialogue (Rao et al., 2021).

At its core, psychological boundaries embody the delicate balance between personal freedom and social responsibility. They remind us that, while interconnected and interdependent, we each hold the right to our mental and emotional space. Respecting these boundaries is fundamental to creating harmonious and thriving societies.

In Conclusion, psychological boundaries are essential for emotional stability and serve as the foundation of healthy relationships and communities. Understanding, respecting, and safeguarding these boundaries is a shared responsibility that requires empathy, clear communication, and ongoing effort. As we navigate modern complexities, let us honor these invisible yet powerful lines that define our humanity.

Spiritual Boundaries

Understanding the intricate development of human societies—from hunter-gatherer communities to complex civilizations—requires exploring multiple dimensions, one of which is spirituality and its boundaries. Spiritual boundaries are not only crucial for maintaining individual inner peace; they also play a vital role in fostering societal cohesion and guiding cultural evolution.

These boundaries provide a framework within which individuals can explore and protect their spiritual beliefs, values, and practices. They serve as invisible yet powerful guidelines, helping to delineate personal spiritual needs while supporting a shared sense of communal identity.

In early societies, spiritual boundaries were often reinforced through rituals, symbols, and collaborative narratives, creating a unified sense of purpose and belonging that helped communities navigate existential questions and collaborative challenges. As societies evolved, these boundaries continued to adapt, reflecting the changing beliefs and values within each culture. The respectful acknowledgement of spiritual boundaries enables individuals to cultivate personal inner peace, while also fostering societal harmony by encouraging mutual respect for diverse spiritual expressions.

Identifying Spiritual Boundaries

Throughout history, human societies have depended on spiritual frameworks to shape their sense of self and community. Although often intangible, spiritual boundaries guide how individuals and groups navigate their existence and find meaning. To identify these boundaries, we can examine personal experiences, communal rituals, and societal norms that provide guidance on what constitutes one's sacred space.

Spiritual boundaries are the lines that define our mental, emotional, and spiritual well-being. They help us distinguish where we end and others begin, creating a clear line between what is spiritually nourishing and what may be draining or invasive.

This demarcation was evident even in early societies, where shamans or spiritual leaders directed communal activities, helping to maintain the collaborative spiritual integrity. This guidance often materialized through rituals, symbols, and shared stories that reinforced these boundary lines in people's minds and hearts (Counted et al., 2022).

These boundaries play an essential role in ensuring that individuals can protect their spiritual well-being while engaging meaningfully with others. They enable people to define their spiritual needs and create a balanced space where personal beliefs can coexist within a larger community.

Consequences of Spiritual Intrusions

When spiritual boundaries are breached—whether intentionally or inadvertently—the consequences can be profound. One of the most immediate effects is the disruption of inner peace. Individuals may experience anxiety, confusion, or a sense of disconnection from their core natural identity. On a broader scale, such intrusions can lead to societal unrest and fragmentation. For instance, the colonial imposition on indigenous spiritual practices historically resulted in cultural upheaval and identity crises, fracturing communities and eroding collaborative resilience.

Spiritual intrusions also impact health. Research shows that the stress and emotional turmoil arising from these breaches can weaken immune function, leading to physical illness. Historically, this pattern was evident in communities subjected to forced assimilation, where individuals faced a loss of cultural and spiritual grounding. This disconnection often correlated with higher rates of mental and physical illnesses, highlighting the essential role of spiritual integrity in maintaining overall well-being (Paradies et al., 2021).

In summary, respecting spiritual boundaries is not just a matter of personal well-being; it is vital for societal harmony and health. When these boundaries are honored, individuals and communities alike can foster resilience, connection, and holistic wellness.

Preserving Spiritual Integrity

Preserving spiritual integrity requires intentionality and effort, particularly in a modern world filled with distractions and demands. To protect our spiritual boundaries, we must first recognize their importance, understanding that they are foundational to our overall well-being.

Here are practical steps to help maintain your spiritual boundaries:

- **Engage in regular self-reflection** to clarify and reinforce what nourishes your spirit.

- **Establish daily practices**—such as meditation or journaling—that keep you grounded and connected to your core values.

- **Respect others' spiritual spaces** by being mindful of their beliefs and practices, fostering a culture of mutual respect and understanding.

- **Set clear limits in relationships and interactions**, openly communicating your needs to maintain spiritual health.

Communal support also plays a pivotal role in preserving spiritual integrity. Societies that create environments where diverse spiritual practices are respected and encouraged tend to experience higher levels of social harmony and cohesion. For instance, encouraging dialogue and understanding across different faith traditions can build bridges rather than walls, contributing to a more inclusive and peaceful society.

Our journey from hunter-gatherer bands to sprawling metropolises is marked by the rise of organized religions and spiritual movements, each offering new layers of meaning and structure to life. Despite the scale and complexity of modern society, the essence of spiritual boundaries remains consistent: they serve as sanctuaries for the soul, nurturing resilience and guiding moral compasses.

When we honor these boundaries, both individually and collaboratively, we foster environments that support well-being, resilience, and mutual respect.

Key Takeaway

Spiritual boundaries are essential for safeguarding our inner peace and maintaining a strong connection with our soul—the essence that sustains us through both wakeful moments and deep slumber. By identifying, respecting, and actively protecting these boundaries, we not only enhance our personal well-being but also contribute to the broader tapestry of communal harmony and societal evolution.

Spiritual integrity, much like any other form of integrity, demands constant vigilance, empathy, and a commitment to mutual respect. In doing so, we embrace both our personal responsibility and the collaborative duty to foster a society where each individual's spiritual space is valued and protected (Counted et al., 2020).

This exploration highlights the importance of balancing personal spiritual health with societal expectations. Our progress as human societies is measured not only by technological advancements or material wealth but by the depth of our spiritual wholeness and the sanctity of our inner lives. By upholding these spiritual boundaries, we advance toward a more harmonious, compassionate world where individual integrity and communal respect thrive in equilibrium.

Human Boundaries: The Pillars of Healthy Interactions

As we trace the evolution of human societies from hunter-gatherer communities to complex civilizations, it becomes evident how fundamental boundary respect is to shaping healthy interactions and fostering societal growth. Physical boundaries have always been crucial, as acknowledging personal space nurtures mutual respect and trust. Effective communication, empathy, and attentiveness enhance our social bonds by honoring everyone's need for personal space.

However, when physical boundaries are violated, discomfort, anxiety, or even trauma can result, eroding trust and straining relationships. This chapter emphasizes the importance of respecting personal space, advocating strategies such as observing non-verbal cues, seeking permission before initiating contact, and honoring verbalized preferences to maintain healthy interactions.

Consistent application of these practices not only supports individual comfort but also promotes collaborative well-being.

Cognitive boundaries, meanwhile, are pivotal for maintaining mental clarity and focus. As we navigate overwhelming amounts of information daily, setting cognitive boundaries helps mitigate stress and boost productivity. Prioritizing tasks, practicing mindfulness, and assertively managing interruptions are essential strategies to protect our mental space. These practices reflect the fact that cognitive efforts have historically been instrumental in developing tools, language, and social cooperation—foundational elements in societal advancement (Stocker et al., 2021).

Psychological boundaries protect emotional health by defining what we accept from others. Understanding personal limits, communicating assertively, and practicing self-care are vital to maintaining these boundaries. Breaches of psychological boundaries can cause emotional distress and strain community harmony, underscoring their importance for both individual well-being and broader societal health.

Spiritual boundaries have historically guided societal norms and rituals, playing a critical role in societal cohesion. Preserving spiritual integrity involves regular self-reflection, grounding practices, and respect for others' spiritual spaces. These boundaries help foster inner peace and mutual respect across diverse spiritual beliefs, enhancing societal harmony.

Considering all these dimensions—physical, cognitive, psychological, and spiritual—demonstrates that maintaining boundaries is essential for human survival and flourishing. As societies evolve, nurturing these boundaries establishes a foundation for healthier interactions and cohesive communities. The consequences of disregarding boundaries are significant, impacting both individual well-being and social harmony (Karremans et al., 2020).

In Conclusion, recognizing and respecting boundaries extends beyond social conventions; it embodies valuing each person's personal space and fostering a culture of safety and respect. By actively incorporating strategies to uphold these boundaries, we contribute to healthier relationships and a more harmonious society. As we continue to advance, balancing progress with empathy and respect remains fundamental to thriving communities.

Chapter 4
The Intersection of Biology and Spirituality

In a world teeming with complexity and diverse experiences, the intersection of biology and spirituality provides a compelling perspective on human existence. This synergy between our biological makeup and spiritual practices has profound implications for our lives, impacting everything from communal bonds to individual well-being. By examining how these elements interact, we gain a deeper understanding of what it means to be fully alive and connected, both individually and collaboratively.

Consider the array of spiritual practices that people engage in—from meditation and mindfulness to community rituals and personal mantras. These activities are far more than cultural artifacts; they have measurable effects on our physical health and mental states. Research, for example, has shown that regular meditation can lower blood pressure, reduce stress hormones, and increase feelings of happiness and contentment.

Likewise, communal rituals provide a sense of belonging and purpose, which are vital for mental health. Our very biology appears to respond positively to these spiritual engagements, suggesting that such practices may be more than just personal or cultural preferences; they may, in fact, serve as essential survival mechanisms. This chapter explores the biological foundations of spirituality, distinguishing them from religious dogma, superstition, and fundamentalism. By examining various spiritual practices, we will consider how these activities contribute to psychological well-being and societal cohesion.

Through empirical evidence and vivid examples, we'll show how spiritual beliefs bolster communal harmony and support individual health. Whether it's the calming effect of meditation or the unifying power of collaborative rituals, this exploration will illuminate the intricate ways in which our biological and spiritual dimensions are interconnected (Van Cappellen et al., 2021).

Ultimately, understanding this relationship can help us see how spirituality, far from being separate from our physical selves, is woven into the very fabric of human survival and thriving.

Words as Bridges

Language, at its core, is an essential component of human interaction. More than a series of sounds escaping our mouths, it is a tool that simplifies the complex tapestry of human emotions and thoughts. By distilling our intentions into words, we create connections that might not have existed otherwise. One of the most vital aspects of language is clarity—being succinct and direct from the outset. This doesn't mean being abrupt or curt; rather, it ensures that our message is clear, leaving little room for misinterpretation.

Consider how much easier it is to navigate challenging conversations when all parties involved understand precisely what's at stake. When intentions are clearly communicated upfront, they lay a foundation of transparency and trust. It's like wiping fog off a windshield—you see where you're headed, and so does everyone else (Keating and Jarvenpaa, 2022).

This brings us to attentive listening—a fundamental component in building meaningful connections through words. Listening is more than hearing; it's about fully engaging with the other person's message without assumptions or interruptions. Misunderstandings often arise when one party projects their own feelings onto someone else's words. Avoiding these pitfalls requires conscious effort, but the rewards are significant.

Imagine two people debating a contentious issue. One might be tempted to interject constantly, challenging every point. But what if, instead, they listened attentively and waited until the other person finished speaking before sharing their perspective? This simple act of patience can transform a heated debate into productive dialogue, fostering mutual respect and understanding.

To achieve effective communication, consider the following guidelines:

- **Avoid making assumptions** about what the other person means.
- **Refrain from interrupting** while they are speaking.
- **Be mindful not to project your own emotions** onto their words.

Creating an environment where all parties feel heard isn't merely an idealistic goal—it's backed by empirical evidence. Studies show that teams practicing active listening outperform those that don't by considerable margins. Conscientious dialogue is key not only in personal relationships but also in professional and societal contexts.

When faced with misunderstanding, the natural inclination may be to jump in hastily with responses that don't address the root of the confusion. However, pausing to acknowledge that you didn't fully grasp what was said and asking open-ended questions for clarification can go a long way. For example, instead of saying, "I don't get it," you could ask, "Could you elaborate on what you meant by…?" This approach allows the speaker to provide additional context, reducing ambiguity and fostering a clearer exchange of ideas (Rosenbaum and Rohn, 2021).

The consequences of vague expressions of misunderstanding cannot be overstated; they can escalate tensions and lead to further miscommunication, derailing otherwise constructive conversations. If you're unclear about a point, it may be more beneficial to continue listening attentively, making mental notes, and saving your questions for when the other person has finished.

Language has unparalleled power in creating bonds and building community. The importance of clear communication and conscientious dialogue cannot be overstated. Educators and psychologists suggest that incorporating these principles into early education could significantly enhance social cohesion and individual psychological well-being. This isn't a theoretical proposition; it's a practice with observable benefits in our daily interactions (Jones and Kahn, 2020).

Imagine the potential for societal improvement if everyone adhered to these communication principles. Civil discourse could become the norm rather than the exception. Public forums—whether physical or digital—could transform into spaces of genuine learning and cooperation instead of arenas for combative rhetoric. In workplaces, teams could operate more harmoniously, achieving greater productivity and innovation.

Words are magical in their ability to forge connections between hearts and minds. When used thoughtfully, they build bridges that span divides of misunderstanding and mistrust, creating strong and meaningful connections. Embracing the power of language means recognizing its capacity to hurt or heal, divide or unite, obscure or illuminate. And it starts with each of us, choosing our words carefully and receiving others' communications with openness and sincerity.

So, the next time you find yourself in conversation, whether casual or profound, remember the pivotal role your words play. In the ever-evolving dance of human connections, let language be your ally—a means to bridge gaps, bring clarity, and nurture the intricate web of relationships that define our shared existence.

Reciprocal Communication

The relationship between biology and spirituality is a fascinating intersection that highlights how our biological wiring influences spiritual experiences—and vice versa. This dynamic is especially evident in reciprocal communication, a foundational element in fostering mutual understanding and harmony.

While boundaries are often thought of as physical—walls, fences, or maps—cognitive, psychological, and spiritual boundaries are equally crucial, though less visible. These boundaries define our sense of self and shape our interactions with others. Just as physical boundaries safeguard personal space, cognitive and psychological boundaries protect our mental well-being and spiritual integrity.

In dialogue, respecting these boundaries is essential. Overstepping them can lead to misunderstandings or emotional distress. For instance, when one person dismisses another's deeply held beliefs, it disrupts communication and damages the trust needed for meaningful exchanges. By honoring each other's cognitive, psychological, and spiritual spaces, we create the foundation for effective and harmonious interactions.

Active listening is a vital component of respectful communication. This goes beyond merely hearing words; it's about genuinely understanding the speaker's message and intent. Active listening creates a receptive environment, allowing individuals to express themselves without fear of judgment or interruption. When you listen actively, you validate the other person's perspective and emotions, which not only improves communication but also deepens connection and enriches relationships (Spataro and Bloch, 2021).

Creating an environment conducive to open dialogue involves adopting an open posture, maintaining eye contact, and using verbal affirmations. Asking clarifying questions and paraphrasing to confirm understanding shows respect for the speaker's cognitive and psychological boundaries, fostering genuine exchanges.

To master active listening:

- **Focus entirely on the speaker,** avoiding distractions.

- **Acknowledge their points** with verbal affirmations like "I understand" or "That makes sense."

- **Reflect back what you've heard** to confirm understanding.

- **Avoid interrupting** or planning your response while they are speaking.

- **Show empathy** through facial expressions and body language.

Reciprocity is also key to maintaining boundaries. Mutual respect in communication is built on the understanding that each person's boundaries are sacrosanct.

When these boundaries are disregarded—such as when someone interrupts or dominates a conversation—it can disrupt the balance necessary for respectful interaction.

When addressing boundary breaches, a gentle approach is essential. By calmly pointing out the issue and suggesting a pause or shift in topic, you maintain the dignity of the conversation and respect both parties involved. Knowing when to terminate a discussion also helps preserve mutual respect and prevents further transgressions.

To uphold reciprocity in boundary maintenance:

- **Be aware of non-verbal cues** indicating discomfort or disengagement.
- **Gently highlight any boundary violations** with statements like "I feel uncomfortable when…"
- **Suggest a break** if the dialogue becomes heated.
- **Use "I" statements** to avoid sounding accusatory and focus on your own perspective.
- **Prioritize resolution over "winning"** to restore harmony.

Reciprocal communication is more than a social nicety; it is a cornerstone of civil discourse. It enables us to navigate complex conversations, resolve conflicts, and build stronger communities. Honoring each other's cognitive, psychological, and spiritual boundaries through active listening and boundary maintenance fosters an atmosphere of mutual respect and understanding (Itzchakov and Kluger, 2022).

Imagine a society where each conversation is marked by such respect, where individuals listen not just to respond but to comprehend fully. In such a world, disagreements would rarely escalate, as everyone would feel valued and understood. Empathy and compassion would become the norm, contributing to greater societal stability and cohesion.

Our biological predispositions toward empathy and cooperation underscore the importance of these practices. Evolution has wired us to thrive in groups, and spirituality often reinforces pro-social behaviors. Practices like meditation, mindfulness, and communal rituals enhance our sense of belonging and well-being, directly impacting individual health and societal harmony.

Integrating these communication principles into our lives doesn't merely improve interactions; it aligns us with our biological and spiritual foundations. Reciprocal communication fosters environments where everyone feels seen, heard, and respected (Khoury et al., 2023).

Reciprocal communication isn't just a tool for individual betterment; it is a building block for a more cohesive, empathetic society. As we refine our ability to listen actively and maintain boundaries respectfully, we contribute to a world where human welfare takes precedence, and economic progress supports this welfare holistically.

Reflecting on these ideas reveals that the interplay between biology and spirituality provides valuable insights into human connection. The principles of reciprocity and active listening are not abstract concepts; they are vital skills rooted in our evolutionary need for community and our spiritual quest for harmony. By embracing these practices, we not only enrich personal relationships but also contribute to a more stable and compassionate society (Kreplin et al., 2021).

Let us commit to fostering reciprocal communication in our daily lives. By listening more, respecting boundaries, and engaging with empathy, we honor the interconnectedness of our biology and spirituality, promoting a world where every voice is heard and each individual thrives.

The Relationship Between Biology and Spirituality: The Exchange of Life-Affirming Energy Through Communication

When we think about conversations, we typically focus on the words spoken and the ideas exchanged. Yet beneath this surface lies a fascinating interplay of energies that deeply influences not only our interactions but also our emotional and physical well-being. These exchanges represent an exchange of life-affirming energy that goes beyond verbal expression, tapping into both our biological and spiritual dimensions.

In every conversation, our body language, tone, and the emotions we convey create an energy field that affects both ourselves and those with whom we engage. Science tells us that our bodies respond to positive and negative interactions on a physiological level—hormones like oxytocin and cortisol can be triggered depending on whether a conversation feels supportive or stressful. Positive interactions tend to increase feelings of happiness and connection, while negative exchanges can lead to stress, anxiety, and even physical health impacts.

This exchange of energy also has a spiritual aspect. When we approach conversations with genuine presence and empathy, we create a sense of connection that transcends words. This connection can be deeply fulfilling, nourishing our inner lives and helping us feel more aligned with our purpose and values. Spiritual practices like mindfulness and active listening amplify this life-affirming energy by encouraging us to be fully present, respect boundaries, and engage with sincerity.

Ultimately, understanding the relationship between biology and spirituality in communication helps us recognize that our conversations are more than just information-sharing. They are dynamic exchanges that can uplift, heal, and foster well-being, reminding us that every interaction holds the potential to contribute positively to both our lives and the lives of others.

How Words Transmit Energy

Words are not merely vessels of meaning; they are dynamic carriers of energy. When we speak, our tone, volume, and choice of words transmit a certain frequency to the listener. This concept is not mystical; it's an empirically observed phenomenon. Studies in psycholinguistics demonstrate that different words and phrases activate varied neural pathways in the brain, influencing our emotions and even physical states.

Consider a time when a compliment lifted your spirits or an argument left you feeling drained. These experiences involve genuine shifts in your psychological and physiological state. Research shows that positive affirmations can lead to increased dopamine levels—the chemical associated with pleasure and reward. Conversely, stressful conversations raise cortisol levels, triggering the body's fight-or-flight response (Moieni and Eisenberger, 2020).

Understanding this biological exchange helps us see how spirituality—viewed here as practices focused on personal and communal well-being outside formal religious structures—can enhance resilience and cohesion. Whether through an uplifting mantra, a supportive conversation, or simple words of kindness, these interactions act as catalysts for positive energy, strengthening communal bonds and bolstering individual morale.

Ultimately, recognizing the power of words in transmitting energy underscores their impact not only on communication but also on our collaborative emotional health and well-being.

Positive vs. Negative Energy Exchanges

Understanding the nuances of energy exchanges allows us to navigate conversations more consciously. Positive energy exchanges are uplifting, encouraging, and constructive, and they bring not only good feelings but tangible health benefits, such as reduced stress and enhanced immune function. For example, engaging in heartfelt, positive dialogue has been shown to lower blood pressure and improve cardiovascular health.

Negative energy exchanges, conversely, can be detrimental. Constant criticism, hostility, or negativity seeps into our psyche and body, leading to increased anxiety, elevated stress hormones, and weakened immune responses. This does not mean we should avoid difficult conversations—conflict is a natural part of human interaction—but rather emphasizes the need for mindful engagement (Kiecolt-Glaser et al., 2022).

An enlightening study in social psychology found that couples who communicated with empathy and positive affirmations had significantly lower stress markers compared to those who engaged in negative exchanges.

This underscores how vital compassionate communication is for sustaining relationships and supporting individual well-being.

By fostering positive exchanges, we can create interactions that are both nourishing and supportive, reinforcing the profound connection between our biological health and our social and spiritual lives.

Maintaining Balanced Energy in Conversations

Balancing energy in conversations requires intentionality and mindfulness. Here are some practical guidelines to help you achieve this equilibrium:

- **Start with Awareness:** Before engaging in significant conversations, take a moment to assess your own emotional state. This awareness enables you to regulate your energy, creating a more centered approach to the exchange.

- **Listen Actively:** True listening goes beyond hearing words; it involves attuning to the speaker's tone, body language, and underlying emotions. Active listening validates the other person's experience, setting the stage for a positive and balanced exchange.

- **Use Affirmative Language: Choose** words that uplift rather than criticize. Simple affirmations like "I understand" or "That sounds challenging" acknowledge the other person's feelings without judgment, promoting a supportive atmosphere.

- **Mind Your Tone and Body Language**: Non-verbal cues can enhance or undermine the energy conveyed by your words. Ensure that your tone and body language align with your intent, helping to maintain a harmonious interaction.

- **Set Boundaries:** If a conversation becomes overly draining, it's okay to pause and suggest revisiting it later. Setting boundaries allows you to manage your energy without adding stress, preserving the balance for future interactions.

Implementing these practices can elevate everyday conversations, turning them into powerful avenues for spiritual and emotional growth. By consciously managing the energy we emit and absorb, we contribute to a healthier and more connected community, enriching our collaborative well-being.

Key Takeaway: Conversations go beyond the simple exchange of information; they are essential conduits of energy that profoundly impact our mental and physical states. Adopting a balanced approach to these exchanges is not just beneficial but vital to our collaborative well-being.

By recognizing the deeper currents of energy flowing through our words, we create pathways for more meaningful, spiritually enriching interactions that uplift both ourselves and those around us.

Signs of Healthy Communication

Healthy communication is a fundamental pillar of a well-functioning, cohesive society. It bridges gaps between individuals, fosters respect, and nurtures understanding, paving the way for effective collaboration and constructive conflict resolution.

Here's a look at what constitutes healthy communication and how it can be cultivated to enhance both personal and communal well-being:

- **Active Listening:** Healthy communication begins with truly listening. Active listening means giving full attention, not interrupting, and showing genuine interest in what the other person is saying. This respect for the speaker's perspective establishes a foundation of trust and openness.

- **Clarity and Honesty:** Effective communication is clear and direct, avoiding ambiguity. Honesty in expressing thoughts, feelings, and intentions helps reduce misunderstandings and builds credibility.

- **Empathy and Understanding**: Healthy communication involves empathy—seeking to understand the other person's feelings and experiences. When we communicate with empathy, we create a supportive environment where all parties feel valued and heard.

The following approach is the key:

- **Respectful Language:** Using respectful and positive language, even in disagreements, fosters a safe environment for expression. Healthy communication avoids belittling, dismissive, or overly critical remarks, promoting mutual respect.

- **Constructive Feedback:** Healthy communication includes constructive feedback rather than criticism. When offering feedback, framing it as supportive advice rather than pointing out flaws encourages growth and minimizes defensiveness.

- **Non-Verbal Cues:** Communication isn't just verbal; body language, facial expressions, and tone are all integral. Healthy communication aligns non-verbal cues with verbal messages, ensuring consistency and authenticity.

- **Patience and Open-Mindedness:** Effective communicators remain patient, giving each other time to articulate thoughts and welcoming diverse perspectives. Open-mindedness allows for a richer, more inclusive dialogue.

Cultivating these elements of healthy communication can significantly enhance personal interactions and strengthen communal bonds.

In fostering active listening, empathy, and clarity, we build an environment where mutual respect and understanding flourish, laying the groundwork for a society marked by collaboration, cohesion, and shared growth.

Indicators of Respectful Communication

Respectful communication is the foundation of any meaningful interaction. It involves actively listening and valuing the other person's perspective, even when it differs from our own. By engaging in respectful communication, you validate others' feelings and experiences, enhancing mutual understanding and trust.

Here are key indicators of respectful communication:

Active Listening: Show genuine engagement with the speaker by making eye contact, nodding, or using affirmations like "I see" or "That's interesting." These cues demonstrate that you are fully present in the conversation.

Non-verbal Cues: Your body language should convey openness and attentiveness. Avoid crossing your arms or looking away, as these gestures can seem dismissive.

Empathy: Try to understand the emotions behind the words. Empathy can elevate a simple exchange into a more meaningful connection, fostering a deeper relational bond.

Avoiding Judgment: Hold off on evaluating or forming an opinion immediately. Instead, focus on fully understanding the other person's message before making judgments.

Listen without planning your response: Focus entirely on the other person's words rather than pre-formulating a reply while they are speaking.

For those wanting to cultivate respectful communication, consider the following steps:

- **Validate feelings:** Acknowledge the other person's emotions by responding in ways that affirm their experience.

- **Minimize distractions**: Put aside distractions, such as phones or television, to show that you are prioritizing the conversation.

By practicing these indicators of respectful communication, you create a foundation of trust and openness, fostering more authentic and meaningful connections.

The Importance of Not Interrupting

Interruptions can quickly derail a conversation, leading to misunderstandings and frustration. When someone interrupts, it often conveys that they value their point over the speaker's, which can erode trust and respect. By consciously avoiding interruptions, you give the speaker the space to fully express their thoughts—a crucial practice, especially in discussions involving complex or emotionally charged issues. How can we achieve this?

- **Practice Patience:** Wait until the other person has finished speaking before you respond. Taking a moment to pause before jumping in can help maintain the flow of respectful communication.

- **Use Non-Verbal Cues:** If you need to interject, consider non-verbal signals like subtly raising a hand to indicate your intent to speak without disrupting their train of thought.

- **Be Aware of Power Dynamics:** Interruptions can be more common among those who hold more power in a relationship or conversation. Staying mindful of this dynamic can help balance dialogue and create a more equitable space for all voices.

Letting someone finish their thought is a simple yet powerful way to show respect for their viewpoint. This practice fosters more productive, respectful conversations, ultimately building a foundation of trust and understanding.

Maintaining Focus and Clarity

In our fast-paced world, conversations can easily splinter into multiple directions, making it challenging to resolve the original topic.

Maintaining focus and clarity in communication ensures that the conversation stays on track, allowing each party to be heard and understood.

To Maintain Focus:

- **Set Intention:** Begin by clearly stating the purpose of the conversation. This helps orient everyone and keeps the dialogue focused on the primary goal.

- **Summarize Regularly:** Periodically summarizing key points helps clarify ideas and ensures that everyone is aligned.

- **Stay on Topic:** While it's tempting to explore related issues, try to stick to the main subject until it's thoroughly discussed.

- To Maintain Clarity:

- **Use Simple Language:** Avoid jargon or complex terms that may confuse the listener. Simplicity enhances understanding.

- **Be Direct but Kind:** State your points clearly and respectfully. Directness coupled with kindness promotes transparency and trust.

- **Ask for Feedback:** Encourage questions if something is unclear. This invites dialogue and helps ensure clarity throughout the conversation.

Healthy communication respects boundaries and fosters understanding. By engaging respectfully, avoiding interruptions, and maintaining focus and clarity, we create an environment where meaningful, productive dialogue can flourish. This practice enhances communal cohesion and psychological well-being, ultimately contributing to societal stability and individual health (Keating et al., 2023).

Every interaction is an opportunity to practice and refine these skills. Whether discussing everyday matters or engaging in deeper, spiritual conversations, the principles of respectful communication remain fundamental. They underpin our interactions, promoting harmony and understanding in all aspects of life.

Bridging Biology and Spirituality Through Communication

Exploring the intersection of biology and spirituality reveals a compelling relationship central to human existence. This chapter has examined how spiritual beliefs and practices—distinct from religious doctrines, superstitions, and dogmas—are deeply grounded in our biological makeup, playing a significant role in fostering communal cohesion and psychological well-being.

Revisiting the core premise, the emphasis on clear communication and active listening provides a foundation for understanding this relationship. By respecting cognitive and psychological boundaries in conversations, we create spaces conducive to trust and mutual respect. This approach aligns with biological imperatives for empathy and cooperation, which are essential for both group survival and individual health (Decety and Yoder, 2021).

Reciprocal communication—where boundaries are honored, and voices are genuinely heard—is not merely beneficial but crucial. This exchange strengthens emotional bonds and social harmony, affirming that spiritual practices like mindfulness and communal rituals can have a positive impact on societal stability.

Some readers may wonder how these principles apply in everyday life, particularly within diverse cultural contexts. The challenge lies in consistently implementing these communication strategies despite varying societal norms and personal belief systems. However, the benefits of adopting these practices on a larger scale are significant. A society that prioritizes empathetic listening and respectful dialogue is likely to experience reduced conflict and increased cooperation, nurturing a more cohesive community.

Reflecting on these insights, it becomes evident that the interplay between biology and spirituality offers a valuable framework for understanding human behavior. These communication principles are not just abstract concepts; they are practical tools rooted in our evolutionary predisposition for empathy and our spiritual longing for harmony. Integrating these practices into daily life enhances interactions and aligns us with our inherent capacities for cooperation and compassion (Purzycki et al., 2022).

As we move forward, let us commit to fostering reciprocal communication in all our interactions. By listening more, respecting boundaries, and engaging with empathy, we honor the interconnectedness of our biology and spirituality. This dedication promotes a world where voices are valued, individuals flourish, and communities thrive.

Chapter 5
The Concept of Civilization

Civilization is a term often taken for granted, yet its true meaning eludes many. What truly makes a society civilized? Is it the gleaming skyscrapers that punctuate the skyline, the technological advancements that drive us forward, or something more profound and intangible? To fully understand civilization, we must look beyond material progress and examine the values and principles that underpin a harmonious society. This chapter seeks to unravel these layers, presenting a nuanced exploration of what it means to be genuinely civilized.

Our modern world offers numerous examples illustrating the complex balance between technological advancement and moral responsibility. In cities worldwide, rapid development and innovation coexist with social unrest and ethical dilemmas. Consider social media: it has connected millions, yet it has also created echo chambers, fueled polarization, and even sparked conflicts (Cinelli et al., 2021).

Similarly, advances in artificial intelligence promise to revolutionize industries, yet they raise pressing questions about privacy, job displacement, and ethical AI usage. These scenarios underscore that while technology can propel societies forward, it does not inherently lead to a more humane or ethical world.

In this chapter, we delve into the essence of civilization by examining the interplay between technological progress, moral growth, and social harmony. We will discuss the defining characteristics of a civilized society, emphasizing the importance of ethical and cultural development alongside material achievements.

Through exploring qualities like self-awareness, empathy, conscience, and humility, we aim to show how these attributes contribute to a balanced and thriving community. By understanding these elements, we gain insight into fostering a civilization that values human welfare as much as economic and technological success.

Awakening to Ignorance

Recognizing one's own ignorance is often the first step toward enlightenment and growth. This awakening is not a single moment of realization but an evolving journey requiring deep introspection and a willingness to challenge preconceived notions.

The initial stages of awakening begin as a subtle awareness that there might be more to know than meets the eye. It often starts when we encounter perspectives that differ significantly from our own experiences or beliefs. This can be sparked by reading a thought-provoking book, experiencing cultural differences, or engaging in meaningful conversations with people from diverse backgrounds (Zmigrod et al., 2023).

Here are ways to initiate this stage of awakening:

- **Seek Diverse Perspectives:** Read books, articles, and studies that present differing viewpoints on issues you care about.

- **Engage in Open Conversations:** Talk to people from different backgrounds and listen actively, resisting the urge to judge immediately.

- **Experience Different Cultures:** Travel or immerse yourself in unfamiliar cultural settings to see life through various lenses.

- **Reflect on Challenging Moments:** Consider situations where your assumptions have been questioned and reflect on why these new perspectives resonated.

Engaging in these practices fosters a new layer of self-awareness. This self-awareness is essential in recognizing one's ignorance because it reveals the limits of our knowledge. By observing our thoughts, emotions, and reactions, we start to notice patterns that may be rooted in misconceptions or gaps in understanding. Self-awareness also requires humility—a recognition that we don't have all the answers and that our current understanding is always evolving.

To enhance self-awareness, consider these steps:

- **Journal Regularly:** Document your thoughts, emotions, and responses to new information or challenging interactions.

- **Practice Mindfulness:** Techniques like meditation help you understand your internal responses more clearly.

- **Seek Constructive Feedback:** Invite honest insights from trusted friends or mentors to uncover blind spots.

- **Question Your Beliefs:** Regularly examine why you hold certain beliefs. Are they based on evidence, tradition, or personal experience?

With self-awareness comes a deeper journey from ignorance to understanding, a process characterized by continuous learning and reassessment. This path is iterative; as we encounter new evidence and experiences, we refine our knowledge.

Strategies to foster understanding include:

- **Adopt a Curious Mindset:** Approach learning with curiosity, not judgment. Be open to ideas that may challenge your existing beliefs.

- **Develop Critical Thinking Skills:** Analyze the quality of information sources and the validity of arguments presented.

- **Join Learning Communities:** Surround yourself with others who value lifelong learning and intellectual growth.

- **Embrace Discomfort:** Growth sometimes involves confronting uncomfortable truths about yourself or the world.

This journey is personal and unique to each individual, and it's not always linear. Moments of confusion, frustration, and doubt are natural and necessary, signaling growth.

Awakening to our own ignorance also fosters empathy and compassion. Recognizing our limitations helps us become more tolerant of others' mistakes and misunderstandings. We start to appreciate the complexity of human behavior and society, moving beyond simple, black-and-white judgments.

In a societal context, this journey contributes to what it means to be civilized. A civilized society embraces diversity of thought, promotes continuous learning, and encourages empathy and cooperation. Technological and material progress hold little value without moral and ethical growth (Page, 2020).

By prioritizing ethical and cultural development, we ensure that progress benefits everyone, not just a select few. This balance between economic advancement and human welfare reflects the core values of a truly civilized society.

In summary, the journey of awakening to one's ignorance begins with exposure to diverse perspectives and deepens through self-awareness and continuous learning. This process not only enriches our understanding but also fosters a more compassionate and empathetic society. By embracing this journey, we contribute to a civilization that values ethical growth and social harmony alongside technological and material advancement.

The Journey to Consciousness

Developing consciousness is a journey that every truly civilized society must undertake. It involves exploring our inner worlds, reflecting on our experiences, and transcending the ego, which ultimately leads us toward enlightenment and harmony. This chapter outlines the essential steps in this journey, illustrating how they contribute to personal growth and a more ethically grounded society.

The first step toward consciousness is **self-awareness**. Recognizing and understanding your own thoughts, emotions, and behaviors forms the foundation for deeper consciousness. Without self-knowledge, progress is limited.

Practices like meditation and journaling cultivate self-awareness by allowing us to observe our thoughts without judgment, creating a space for sincere reflection (Wielgosz et al., 2023).

The next phase involves **education—both formal and informal.** Education broadens our perspective, helping us understand different cultures, philosophies, and ways of thinking. This is not limited to academic learning but includes absorbing life lessons from varied sources: books, mentors, experiences, and even our mistakes.

Approaching education with curiosity and openness enables us to challenge preconceptions and embrace wisdom accumulated over centuries.

Building on self-awareness and education, **critical thinking** becomes essential. This phase involves questioning the status quo, examining evidence, and making reasoned judgments. Critical thinking prevents us from accepting information blindly, prompting us instead to sift through data, recognize biases, and form well-rounded opinions based on logic and empirical evidence (Niu et al., 2023).

An equally vital aspect of developing consciousness is **empathy.** This journey is not solely intellectual; it demands emotional intelligence as well. Empathy enables us to connect with others, understand their struggles, and respond with compassion. Practices like active listening and being present in conversations cultivate empathy, an often-overlooked trait in a society that sometimes values technological advancement over human connection. A truly civilized society recognizes that empathy bridges divides and fosters unity.

Inward reflection plays a pivotal role in this journey. By setting aside time for introspection, we gain insight into our reactions and behaviors, identifying patterns and uncovering core values. Reflection allows us to analyze our responses to various situations, guiding us toward self-improvement. Steps for practicing inward reflection:

- **Create Quiet Space:** Set aside time in a quiet place for uninterrupted introspection.

- **Reflect Daily:** Regularly review your interactions and experiences, asking yourself why you reacted in certain ways and what lessons you can draw.

- **Document Thoughts:** Journaling helps solidify your understanding and track personal growth.

- **Identify Patterns:** Recognize recurring themes in your reflections, which may reveal deeper insights about your beliefs and motivations.

- One of the most challenging aspects of attaining consciousness is overcoming the **ego and shedding false identities**. The ego often creates facades that mask our true selves, leading us to seek validation from external sources. To transcend the ego, one must first recognize it and understand its influence.

Steps for overcoming the ego:

- **Cultivate Humility:** Acknowledge that you don't have all the answers and remain open to learning from others.

- **Practice Self-Compassion:** Accept that mistakes are part of growth, fostering self-kindness over harsh self-criticism.

- **Detach from Societal Expectations:** Focus on who you truly are, rather than who you feel you should be based on external standards.

- **Engage in Authentic Pursuits:** Invest time in activities that nourish your genuine self, such as creative endeavors, volunteering, or spending time in nature.

- **False identities** often arise from societal labels, occupations, or accomplishments. While these aspects may contribute to our sense of self, they should not define us entirely. Stripping away these layers reveals our core essence and purpose.

The journey to consciousness also involves **disillusionment and revelation of truth,** where individuals begin to question previously held beliefs and assumptions. This phase often arises after experiencing profound truths, challenging life events, or "rites of passage." Disillusionment is essential as it propels individuals toward deeper understanding and meaning in their lives. Through introspection, they confront uncomfortable truths about themselves and the world, gradually unveiling the lies they've told themselves, the fears they've hidden, and the desires they've suppressed. This journey, requiring considerable autonomy, cannot be rushed or imposed but must emerge from a sincere desire to grow and evolve (Ryan and Deci, 2020).

As consciousness deepens, individuals naturally prioritize values that favor human welfare over material gain. They begin to seek fulfillment in positively contributing to their communities, a perspective that ripples outward, influencing societal norms and prompting systemic change toward these higher ideals.

A truly civilized society is not just marked by its technological advancements or economic prosperity but by the moral and ethical development of its members. The balance between technological progress and cultural growth is delicate but essential; material advancements should serve as tools to enhance human welfare rather than overshadow it.

To conclude, the path to achieving consciousness is a profound journey encompassing self-awareness, education, critical thinking, empathy, inward reflection, and the transcendence of ego and false identities. As individuals undergo this transformation, they embody the principles of a civilized society, paving the way for a harmonious and enlightened world. By embracing this inward journey, we collaboratively move closer to realizing our highest potential and fostering a civilization rooted in ethical and cultural growth.

Conscience as a Guide

At the core of defining a civilized society lies the role of conscience in guiding behavior. Conscience is more than an inner voice nudging us towards right or wrong; it is a deeply ingrained sense of moral responsibility, cultivated through self-awareness and empathy. Serving as our internal compass, conscience steers us toward ethical conduct and societal harmony.

Conscience functions as a self-regulating mechanism, thriving on awareness of ignorance, consciousness, and humility. Unlike guilt, which often arises from regret or self-reproach, a well-developed conscience promotes proactive behavior rooted in understanding and empathy. While guilt is a reaction to having done something wrong, the essence of conscience is understanding why an action is wrong and striving to avoid it in the future. This distinction is crucial, as genuine compassion stems from empathy—the ability to relate deeply to others' experiences—rather than pity, which is often superficial and rooted in guilt.

Consider the feelings evoked when witnessing someone in distress. If these feelings are based solely on guilt for not experiencing similar hardships, they lack the depth and authenticity needed to inspire meaningful action. However, if they are born out of empathy and a true appreciation for another's emotions and circumstances, they become a powerful driver for conscientious behavior. Authentic compassion leads to action, while compassion rooted in guilt often stops at sentimentality without genuine effort to create change (Bloom, 2021).

What does acting conscientiously look like in practice? Imagine a corporate leader who prioritizes sustainability, not just because it's trendy or mandated by regulations, but from a genuine concern for the planet and future generations. This leader implements recycling programs, invests in renewable energy, and champions fair trade practices, driven by a conscience that recognizes the broader impact of business decisions on global ecosystems and societies.

Similarly, consider a teacher who spends extra hours tutoring struggling students. This teacher's actions aren't motivated by additional pay or recognition; their conscience drives them. They understand that each student's success contributes to a better society, and this realization propels them to go the extra mile. Such teachers feel a deep connection to their students' challenges and potential, inspiring their dedication.

Another example is the individual who consistently volunteers at shelters or food banks. This person may not have experienced hunger or homelessness firsthand, yet they act out of profound empathy and responsibility toward those in need. Their conscience quietly fuels their sustained efforts to support others' welfare, demonstrating that conscientious living extends beyond grand gestures to daily acts of kindness and solidarity (Batson et al., 2022).

The roots of conscience lie in awareness of our ignorance, the cultivation of compassion, and the awakening of consciousness. This triad forms the foundation of a moral compass that guides our actions. Recognizing our limitations and embracing empathy allows us to move beyond words and sentiments to actions with real impact. A well-developed conscience urges us to walk the talk, translating noble ideas into meaningful actions.

When individuals lack this moral compass, society suffers. Policies driven solely by economic growth, for example, often lead to inequality, environmental harm, and social unrest. In contrast, policies informed by a collaborative conscience balance economic interests with the welfare of all citizens, promoting a more harmonious and equitable society. Government and corporate collaborations, guided by public interest, can create lasting positive change. For instance, partnerships focused on improving healthcare access can significantly enhance quality of life for underserved populations, driven by a commitment to compassionate progress.

Conscience is effective only when we act upon it. An individual may hold strong ethical beliefs, but without conscientious actions, these beliefs remain dormant. Here, personal responsibility intersects with societal support. While each person must strive to contribute meaningfully, society must also ensure safety nets for those facing hardships. This dual approach ensures everyone has an opportunity to participate in a thriving community (Han et al., 2021).

Studies reveal that conscientious actions positively impact communities and workplaces. Employees who perceive their workplaces as ethically responsible report higher levels of job satisfaction, productivity, and loyalty. Likewise, communities known for charitable activities experience greater social cohesion and lower crime rates, underscoring how collaborative conscientious behavior enhances societal well-being.

Ultimately, a well-developed conscience is essential for guiding ethical and moral behavior. It encourages us to act with integrity, compassion, and foresight, considering the impact of our actions on others. This internal guide helps us navigate complex situations, ensuring that technological and material progress do not overshadow our moral responsibilities (Gond et al., 2021).

In cultivating conscience, we cultivate a more civilized society. One where technological achievements are matched by moral growth, and social harmony is achieved through a commitment to the greater good. By embracing empathy, recognizing our limitations, and taking ethical action, we create a balanced civilization that values human welfare above mere economic success. This is the essence of being truly civilized—nurturing a conscience that not only guides us but uplifts those around us, paving the way for a more harmonious world.

The Role of Humility

Humility stands as a cornerstone of personal and societal growth. It's a quality that not only fuels individual betterment but also enriches the community. Imagine embarking on a lifelong journey of learning, only to realize there's still so much left to discover. This acknowledgment of ignorance might feel daunting, even exposing vulnerability. But within this openness lies transformative potential: the willingness to say, "I do not know," creates space for genuine growth and understanding.

In embracing our limitations, we allow new knowledge to fill the gaps in our understanding, welcoming insights from others that shape a more complete perspective. Humility acts as a safeguard against arrogance, grounding us and fostering authentic, meaningful interactions. It breaks down the walls of presumption, opening doors to deeper connections with the world around us.

Consider, for instance, the lives of trailblazers in science and the arts. Their achievements were underscored by humility, which they treated as an essential component of their journey. Albert Einstein, despite his revolutionary contributions, spoke of the vast mysteries he had yet to understand. His remark, "The more I learn, the more I realize how much I don't know," highlights humility's vital role in inquiry and discovery. Similarly, physicist Erwin Schrödinger never shied away from acknowledging the limits of his knowledge, a perspective that enabled him to approach quantum mechanics with a questioning mind. Their admissions of ignorance did not obstruct their progress; rather, they served as powerful catalysts for breakthroughs (Zmigrod et al., 2023).

Einstein's intellectual openness led him to rethink fundamental physics concepts, ultimately developing the theory of relativity. By acknowledging what he didn't know, he ventured into new scientific frontiers. Schrödinger's humble exploration of quantum mechanics allowed him to present thought experiments that redefined contemporary science, pushing boundaries and inviting fresh perspectives on wave-particle duality. These examples reveal that acknowledging ignorance can be a profound driver of innovation and insight across fields.

Humility's influence extends beyond intellectual realms—it impacts our overall well-being. Embracing humility reminds us that we are part of a broader ecosystem, interconnected with others and the environment. This mindset encourages us to prioritize collaborative welfare over individual gain, fostering empathy and cooperation. By recognizing our limits and seeking assistance when needed, we improve our mental and emotional health, creating a culture where others feel safe to do the same.

In personal relationships, humility builds trust and mutual respect. Admitting faults or a lack of knowledge without fear of judgment strengthens bonds and fosters understanding. This collaborative support becomes a safety net, allowing people to navigate difficult times with confidence and resilience. In this sense, humility acts as societal glue, holding communities together even amidst challenges.

On a larger scale, humility is essential for ethical growth and balance. It propels us to seek knowledge while remaining mindful of our limitations. As our wisdom expands, so does our capacity for compassion and understanding towards others (Krumrei-Mancuso, 2023).

Humility also shapes decision-making, particularly in balancing economic growth with human welfare. It encourages leaders to value human well-being over pure material success, prompting policymakers to weigh the social impacts of their actions. For instance, in healthcare or housing reforms, a humble approach would prioritize accessibility and equity, ensuring that progress benefits all, not just a select few.

Fostering humility involves adopting a mindset of lifelong learning. Approach each day with curiosity and a readiness to learn. Engage with diverse perspectives, allowing your assumptions to be challenged. When faced with gaps in knowledge, admit them openly and seek answers. Practicing gratitude regularly for the contributions of others also reinforces humility, reminding us of the collaborative efforts that sustain society (Oc et al., 2022).

In professional environments, humility manifests through collaboration, openness to feedback, and valuing all team members' input, regardless of rank. Leaders who model humility create inclusive spaces where each voice is heard, encouraging innovation without fear of mistakes (Ren et al., 2022).

Ultimately, embracing humility transforms our individual journeys and radiates outward, impacting our communities and society. It involves balancing confidence in our abilities with the wisdom to recognize our limits, cultivating an environment where both technological advancement and moral growth flourish. As we journey forward, let humility be our guide, reminding us that true strength lies in acknowledging our imperfections and striving for growth. Through humility, we can build a world where empathy, respect, and ethical integrity form the foundation of sustainable progress and genuine human connection.

Synthesizing Civilized Values

In this chapter, we explored the essential qualities that shape a truly civilized society. We examined how genuine progress requires a harmonious balance between technological advancement and moral and ethical growth. By investigating key concepts like ignorance, consciousness, conscience, and humility, we've established a framework for understanding what it means to be authentically civilized.

Reflecting on our earlier discussions about awakening to ignorance and cultivating self-awareness, it's evident that these initial stages form the foundation for personal and societal evolution. Recognizing our own limitations and challenging our preconceived notions isn't just an intellectual pursuit—it's a vital step toward empathy, compassion, and meaningful human connections.

This journey allows us to see beyond our own perspectives, fostering deeper appreciation for the diversity of human experience. The pursuit of knowledge, guided by continuous learning and critical thinking, should be a lifelong endeavor. Education—whether formal or through life's varied experiences—broadens our worldview and enriches our understanding of cultures, philosophies, and ideas.

However, enlightenment is only meaningful when we apply our knowledge ethically, with conscience as our guide. Acting conscientiously is what truly defines civilized behavior, as it aligns our actions with principles that benefit both individuals and communities.

Overcoming the ego and shedding false identities can be challenging, but it is a necessary step toward authentic self-awareness and empathy. The ego often stands in the way of genuine human connection, promoting external validation over meaningful contribution. Embracing humility allows us to recognize that our worth lies in our relationships and contributions to society, rather than in superficial accolades. Admitting ignorance is not a sign of weakness; rather, it opens the door to greater wisdom and integrity (Krumrei-Mancuso et al., 2020).

The consequences of ignoring these principles are profound. When material progress is pursued at the expense of ethical considerations, society suffers. Issues like inequality, environmental degradation, and social unrest arise from misplaced priorities. In contrast, a society that values human welfare as highly as technological advancement fosters equity, sustainability, and collaborative well-being.

Ultimately, the essence of civilization is found in a balanced approach where scientific and economic progress is matched by moral and cultural growth. Cultivating conscience and humility within ourselves isn't just a personal journey; it contributes to a broader collaborative movement toward a more enlightened and harmonious world. The question remains: How can each of us continue to uphold and nurture these values in our daily lives and communities, ensuring that our progress as a society is inclusive and truly holistic?

Chapter 6
Fostering Localized Grassroots Initiatives

Imagine a world where communities, rather than large governmental entities, drive societal progress. Picture a neighborhood uniting to address local challenges, with individuals collaborating because they care deeply about their shared spaces and common future. This vision of grassroots action is not only feasible but has proven consistently effective. From modest recycling programs in small towns to community gardens feeding people in need, these localized efforts often achieve tangible results more swiftly and sustainably than sprawling centralized systems can (Enarsson, Hinton, and Borgström, 2024).

Local Problems, Local Solutions

The effectiveness of grassroots initiatives lies in recognizing that local issues demand local solutions. Large governments frequently struggle with inefficiency and oversight, impeded by bureaucratic complexities that hinder fast response times. When responsibilities disperse across multiple officials and departments, accountability can fall through the cracks—a phenomenon often referred to as the "Diffusion of Responsibility." In contrast, neighborhood coalitions can swiftly mobilize resources and support during crises, driven by a personal commitment to their immediate surroundings (Liu et al., 2020).

Grassroots Empowerment and Community Engagement

Grassroots movements tap into the power of local activism. History reveals that transformative societal shifts often begin at the community level, where people feel the direct impact of pressing concerns. Local initiatives excel because they can adapt quickly to the needs of their constituents without the delays common in large-scale governmental programs (Manzini and Rizzo, 2021).

Genuine engagement is essential for any healthy society. When citizens participate in governance, policy-making, and problem-solving, they build trust and a sense of ownership. Practical ways to foster this engagement include:

- Creating safe, open platforms for dialogue (town halls, online forums).
- Ensuring transparency in decision-making processes.
- Encouraging volunteerism to strengthen accountability and collective pride.
- Providing education and resources to support community-led solutions.
- Establishing citizen advisory boards to incorporate local insights.

When communities feel heard and valued, they become more inclined to collaborate, which contributes to overall social advancement.

Building Robust Local Networks

Developing effective grassroots movements requires strategies that nurture local leadership and alliances. Key steps include:

- **Identifying common goals:** Unite around urgent regional concerns.

- **Cultivating leadership skills:** Offer mentorship and training to emerging leaders.

- **Forging partnerships:** Collaborate with local businesses, schools, and organizations to pool resources and expertise.

- **Leveraging digital tools:** Use social media, newsletters, and online apps to coordinate and communicate.

- **Setting up feedback loops:** Regularly evaluate progress, celebrate wins, and refine tactics.

Connected networks generate lasting impact. When community-centered groups partner with similar movements, their collective momentum addresses social, economic, and environmental issues at multiple scales—from local to global (Bianchi and Ginelli, 2023).

Enhancing Society Through Decentralization

Grassroots efforts can effectively complement—and sometimes outperform—large government responses, especially in crisis situations. While centralized structures have a place in policymaking and resource allocation, they often lack the agility and immediate urgency that smaller, localized groups demonstrate (Pleyers, 2020).

For instance, when natural disasters strike, local organizations and nonprofits often arrive first, leveraging local knowledge and personal commitment to deliver rapid assistance. Their decentralized approach speeds up both immediate relief and long-term recovery, a contrast to the slower gears of extensive bureaucratic systems.

Ultimately, governments and corporations still play a role: with streamlined processes and improved accountability, they can support grassroots endeavors rather than obstruct them.

By collaborating with decentralized initiatives and minimizing bureaucratic barriers, these larger institutions become true allies in grassroots-led change.

Connecting Communities on a Broader Scale

Grassroots movements achieve greater impact when they collaborate nationally. By linking with other decentralized groups, local initiatives can share resources, unify messaging, and amplify their collective voice.

Digital communication platforms and regular discussion forums can enable representatives from different regions to exchange success stories, coordinate large-scale campaigns, and maintain focus on pressing communal goals (Avelino et al., 2020).

A well-documented example is environmental advocacy. Community groups aiming to reduce plastic waste may start with small-scale beach cleanups or local partnerships to eliminate single-use plastics. As these local projects connect—often through social media—the cumulative effect can influence state or national policy (Mihaylov and Perkins, 2023).

Resource and Best Practice Sharing

A hallmark advantage of decentralization is the capacity for autonomous operation alongside productive cooperation. Grassroots movements benefit from pooling insights and resources:

- **Regional Hubs:** Central points of coordination that facilitate training, resource sharing, and mentorship.

- **Mentorship Programs:** Pairing nascent initiatives with more seasoned organizations supports knowledge transfer and skill-building.

- **Digital Collaboration Tools:** Cloud-based storage and forums foster real-time project updates and accessible shared content.

- **Collective Funding Campaigns:** By jointly raising funds, multiple movements can tackle larger projects, broadening their overall impact.

Local funding sources—community grants, donations, and grassroots fundraisers—also help these movements retain their authenticity and avoid the influence of outside interests.

Advantages Over Centralized Structures

Decentralized networks excel in responsiveness, adaptability, and accountability. Large bureaucratic entities often suffer from sluggish processes and repeated references to "Diffusion of Responsibility," where accountability thins across numerous oversight layers. In contrast, grassroots organizations respond swiftly, especially in emergencies, and directly shoulder responsibility for local welfare (Ribot, 2002).

Rather than displacing government, grassroots efforts push centralized bodies to streamline processes, minimize red tape, and forge alliances with decentralized actors. This balance ensures that policy frameworks and major funding channels work in harmony with local autonomy.

A National Framework for Grassroots Collaboration

To drive tangible national outcomes, decentralized movements can adopt structured yet flexible alliances:

- **National Networks:** Formalize alliances that unite local efforts behind common causes (e.g., healthcare, education, housing).

- **Representative Committees:** Include diverse regional voices to ensure decisions reflect on-the-ground realities.

- **Periodic Workshops:** Offer spaces where participants can strategize, learn from shared experiences, and celebrate achievements.

- **Accountability Mechanisms:** Use transparent reporting to track achievements, financial data, and ongoing challenges.

Through such collaboration, grassroots groups can address complex issues on both a local and national scale. They retain the authenticity of local engagement while benefiting from wider influence and scope (Tormos-Aponte and García-López, 2022).

Regional and Global Ripple Effects

Scaling decentralized efforts regionally and nationally spurs broader societal gains. When grassroots movements share experiences, successes, and solutions, they form a resilient network capable of confronting large-scale problems like environmental threats or inadequate healthcare systems.

In agriculture, for instance, one community's trial-and-error discoveries about sustainable farming can help a neighboring region facing similar climate-related challenges. Both communities evolve through mutual support, demonstrating how small-scale efforts can collectively achieve substantial outcomes (Šūmane et al., 2021).

As these alliances expand, their ideas and results can inspire policy changes, contributing to national discourse and elevating community priorities. This "ripple effect" underscores the transformative potential of grassroots networks that operate independently yet remain connected by overarching values of inclusivity, sustainability, and justice.

Minimizing Government Overreach by Strengthening the Local

Oversized government bureaucracies often become sluggish, riddled with inefficiencies. While elected officials engage in campaign-related activities—fundraising, recruiting volunteers, and ensuring reelection—vital governance tasks can suffer. Thus, civic needs like disaster relief, healthcare reform, or education upgrades remain on hold, overshadowed by institutional inertia (Kapucu and Garayev, 2021).

Grassroots movements anchored in local knowledge can fill these gaps. They act swiftly and concretely—establishing community health clinics, coordinating volunteer emergency responses, or forging alliances to improve local housing. When direct observation of improvements is possible, leaders become accountable to community members in ways that large-scale officials often are not (Ansell and Gash, 2021).

Toward a Balanced Model

A balanced social architecture harnesses the best of both worlds. Governments can offer legislative frameworks, oversight, and resources without smothering local initiatives beneath cumbersome processes. Decentralized networks, for their part, maintain the autonomy, responsiveness, and community-level insight essential for truly equitable progress (De Weger et al., 2023).

In this mixed model:

- **Government**: Sets standards, coordinates broad policy aims, and disburses funding for public welfare.

- **Grassroots Organizations**: Retain agility, local accountability, and adaptability, driving solutions that reflect real community needs.

Focusing on Practical Outcomes

Grassroots partnerships are most effective when they address tangible issues. While visionary goals can be motivating, everyday progress solidifies trust and builds momentum. Communities facing repeated flooding, for example, can cooperate on cost-sharing flood barriers or collectively negotiate insurance and disaster-planning measures. The result is an immediate, verifiable improvement to public safety (Ganz and McKenna, 2022).

By dedicating resources to pressing, real-world concerns, grassroots movements avoid the inefficiencies of grand but untested projects. Instead, they generate measurable results that reinforce broader cooperation efforts.

Collaborating for Regional and National Benefits

Addressing wide-ranging social challenges often demands working beyond city limits. Neighboring communities facing common environmental or economic problems can:

- Conduct joint needs assessments for a fuller picture of overlapping concerns.

- Share technical and financial resources, creating synergy that multiplies each group's efforts.

- Develop localized action plans, ensuring that solutions remain context-specific.

- Remain flexible in governance, permitting swift adjustments to unexpected challenges.

- Evaluate outcomes regularly to keep all participants aligned on shared goals.

By doing so, every community benefits from collective strategies while preserving its autonomy. This approach cultivates resilience, weaving a stronger social fabric that can absorb and adapt to shocks more effectively than any single town or city acting alone.

Conclusion: Cultivating Global Change Through Decentralized, Local Grassroots Collaboration

In looking toward a future defined by inclusivity, adaptability, and shared responsibility, decentralized grassroots movements emerge as catalysts for authentic progress. By anchoring change efforts in local insight and accountability, these initiatives energize communities to address immediate needs while collaborating across wider networks.

The "Diffusion of Responsibility," so prevalent in massive bureaucracies, can be countered by strong local engagement and ownership—leaders in grassroots contexts see firsthand the outcomes of their decisions and cannot hide behind multiple layers of oversight. When these community-based groups merge their efforts regionally and nationally, they form alliances powerful enough to influence policies, shift cultural norms, and improve social, economic, and environmental conditions.

In this vision, governments and large-scale institutions become partners in progress rather than obstacles. By refining their own processes and listening attentively to local advocates, they create a conducive environment in which grassroots movements thrive. This synergy places human welfare at the center, transforming distant policy talk into practical, community-driven action. As these decentralized efforts ripple outward, they pave a path toward a more harmonious, equitable society—one where every person and every neighborhood has both the freedom and the support to flourish.

Chapter 7
Pathways to a Unified Human Society

In a world increasingly interconnected through technology and globalization, the call for a unified human society is more relevant than ever. Imagine a world where empathy and cultural sensitivity are the rule, not the exception—where individuals from diverse backgrounds come together, freely sharing their cultures without imposing superiority or engaging in divisive political discourse. This vision is not merely idealistic; it is an achievable goal through focused, intentional effort. Such a shift begins with a fundamental understanding of one another, embracing our differences while celebrating our shared humanity.

A significant barrier to this unity lies in deeply ingrained cultural divisions that often breed misunderstanding and conflict. These divisions reveal themselves in various ways, from biases based on race or religion to economic disparities that obstruct collaboration. For instance, consider a community event where people from different backgrounds gather to celebrate their cultures.

Often, such events are influenced by government regulations or corporate sponsorships, which can compromise the authenticity of the interactions. Instead of fostering genuine cultural exchange, the event may end up serving organizational agendas, allowing little space for real, heartfelt connections. Additionally, when external interests overshadow local concerns, grassroots efforts may struggle to address issues that genuinely matter to their communities (Vertovec, 2021).

This chapter provides practical strategies to overcome these barriers and cultivate a more unified society. It underscores the role of grassroots movements in bridging cultural divides and advocates for decentralized, community-driven approaches tailored to address local needs. By organizing community-led festivals, collaborative projects, and dialogue circles, individuals can engage in spontaneous, authentic exchanges that foster empathy and mutual understanding.

Moreover, the chapter explores how shared values—like environmental stewardship, economic sustainability, and holistic health—can serve as a unifying foundation for diverse populations. These values offer common ground, allowing different communities to work together toward mutual goals. Through these methods, we lay the groundwork for a world that is more inclusive, equitable, and harmonious (Bhattacharyya et al., 2022).

The Importance of Mutual Understanding

Empathy and cultural sensitivity are indispensable in weaving the fabric of a globally cooperative society. Their importance cannot be overstated; they form the foundation upon which mutual understanding and lasting collaboration can flourish. As our world grows more interconnected, bridging cultural divides becomes not only a moral imperative but also a practical necessity.

One of the most effective strategies for overcoming cultural divides is to foster direct human connections through decentralized, local grassroots movements. Imagine individuals from various cultures coming together, traveling to each other's communities, and participating in joint events. Free from the influence of government regulations or corporate sponsors, these gatherings create an atmosphere where participants can exchange ideas and experiences openly. Such genuine interactions help strip away preconceived notions, building relationships grounded in shared humanity rather than external influences (Pettigrew and Tropp, 2021).

For instance, community-led festivals or collaborative projects focused on arts and culture provide a platform for meaningful dialogue. Engaging in these activities often encourages openness and receptiveness, facilitating easier cultural connections. By creating spaces that allow for unscripted, spontaneous interactions, grassroots initiatives can counteract the undue influence of government or corporate agendas, which often come with political motivations or commercial objectives. Financial backing from politicians or corporate sponsors can sometimes dilute the authenticity of cultural exchanges, underscoring the need for initiatives rooted in community involvement and personal investment (Jepson and Clarke, 2022).

Moreover, grassroots movements enable a decentralized approach to problem-solving, allowing for solutions tailored to the specific needs of each community. For instance, a food cooperative that celebrates diverse culinary traditions or an educational program that includes multicultural perspectives helps break down cultural barriers while fostering a cohesive society. These localized efforts empower individuals to address the issues most relevant to their lives, unburdened by external pressures that may conflict with their community's values.

Here is what you can do to foster an environment of empathy and cultural exchange:

- **Encourage cultural immersion:** Support travel and exchange programs that allow individuals to experience other cultures firsthand, broadening their perspectives and fostering empathy.

- **Organize community festivals or cultural fairs:** Create events where people can share their traditions, stories, and crafts, fostering a genuine appreciation for diversity.

- **Facilitate collaborative projects:** Engage in community-based projects, like gardens or public art installations, that require teamwork across cultural lines.

- **Establish regular dialogue circles:** Form discussion groups focused on cultural exchange and mutual learning, providing a safe space for honest conversations.

- **Avoid reliance on government or corporate funding:** Keep initiatives community-driven to ensure authenticity and genuine connection.

In tandem, establishing shared values is essential for uniting diverse populations within decentralized, community-based grassroots movements. Values like environmental stewardship, economic sustainability, financial equity, and holistic health and well-being are universal concerns around which people from varied backgrounds can rally.

Take environmental stewardship as an example. The importance of preserving natural resources transcends cultural boundaries, as communities worldwide recognize the need to safeguard the planet for future generations. Initiatives like community clean-up drives or conservation projects create tangible ways for individuals to come together for a common cause. Such activities reinforce the importance of environmental preservation while fostering a sense of collaborative responsibility (Krasny and Tidball, 2023).

Economic sustainability and financial equity also offer fertile ground for shared values. Building local economies that prioritize fair trade practices and support small businesses can create more equitable wealth distribution. Community markets or cooperative businesses that focus on locally produced goods not only stimulate the local economy but also cultivate solidarity among residents. When communities promote economic practices that benefit everyone, they establish a more inclusive and resilient social fabric.

Similarly, holistic health and well-being stand as integrative values that unify communities. Programs that prioritize mental health, physical wellness, and emotional resilience bring people together in the pursuit of common goals. Community wellness centers providing services such as yoga, meditation, and nutrition counseling demonstrate how holistic health initiatives can unify a community. By focusing on the well-being of the entire person—body, mind, and spirit—these initiatives help build stronger, more connected communities.

To effectively build shared values within your community, consider the following guidelines:

- **Identify common concerns and interests:** Focus on issues that resonate across cultural lines, ensuring they reflect the community's Shared values.

- **Promote awareness and education**: Use workshops, seminars, and information campaigns to spread knowledge and foster commitment to shared values.

- **Form community-led committees:** Create working groups dedicated to specific causes, ensuring diverse representation from various cultural segments.

- **Celebrate successes collaboratively:** Recognize milestones to reinforce the importance of shared values and strengthen unity.

- **Encourage transparency:** Maintain open communication within initiatives to foster trust and respect among participants.

Empathy and cultural sensitivity allow us to understand and celebrate the complex tapestry of human experience, laying the groundwork for meaningful global cooperation. Grassroots movements play a pivotal role in this process by facilitating direct, unmediated interactions that circumvent the potential distortions introduced by larger institutions. By centering efforts on shared values that prioritize human welfare above pure economic growth, we create a foundation for a more inclusive, balanced, and harmonious world.

As we navigate the intricacies of global society, let us remember that each step toward empathy and mutual understanding brings us closer to genuine unity. Practical strategies that encourage personal responsibility alongside community support can cultivate a world where each individual is valued, and collaborative human welfare takes precedence. In doing so, we honor the diversity of human culture and pave the way for a future grounded in cooperation, compassion, and shared prosperity (Reysen and Katzarska-Miller, 2021).

Fostering Unity Through Empathy and Cultural Sensitivity

In summarizing this chapter, we have examined the essential role of empathy and cultural sensitivity in fostering a unified human society. Through practical, community-driven strategies, we can bridge cultural divides, creating grassroots movements that transcend governmental and corporate influences. These decentralized efforts allow for authentic human connections and foster a sense of shared humanity.

The chapter began with the assertion that mutual understanding is foundational to global cooperation. By centering our approach on empathy and cultural sensitivity, we set the stage for a more cohesive society. This perspective underpins our discussion, emphasizing the need for direct human connections and community-led initiatives to overcome cultural barriers.

Our current stance underscores the critical importance of grassroots movements that remain free from external agendas. Local festivals, collaborative art projects, and decentralized problem-solving initiatives illustrate how communities can engage in meaningful interactions and build genuine relationships. These grassroots exchanges are instrumental in dismantling preconceptions and fostering a deeper understanding across different cultural backgrounds.

However, readers should be mindful of potential challenges. One significant concern is ensuring that these initiatives remain authentic and are not co-opted by larger entities with ulterior motives. Government or corporate financial involvement can sometimes skew the purpose and authenticity of cross-cultural exchanges, undermining the original goal of fostering genuine mutual understanding (Smith and Smythe, 2022).

On a broader scale, the consequences of neglecting empathy and cultural sensitivity can be severe. A lack of mutual understanding risks widening divisions, potentially leading to societal fragmentation and conflict. Thus, it is essential to advocate for and participate in community-based movements that nurture genuine human connections and shared values.

Ending on an open-ended note, it is crucial to reflect continuously on how we, as individuals and communities, can better engage in practices that promote empathy and understanding. Every step taken toward bridging cultural divides brings us closer to a global society marked by cooperation, compassion, and shared prosperity. Transformation begins at the grassroots level, reminding us that every individual effort contributes to the larger goal of unity. As we progress, let us consider how our actions today will shape the harmonious world we aspire to create.

The Future of Human Civilization

As we stand on the threshold of a new era, human civilization faces both unprecedented challenges and boundless opportunities. The future ahead, shaped by the forces of climate change, technological transformation, and persistent global inequities, demands a collaborative effort to steer humanity toward a sustainable and resilient path. This chapter aims to provide a comprehensive overview of the strategies, innovations, and shared values that could pave the way for a brighter tomorrow.

Climate Change and Its Global Impact

The accelerating impact of climate change is visible in our daily lives: from rising temperatures and melting ice caps to increasingly erratic weather patterns that disrupt ecosystems and human livelihoods. These changes are not just environmental concerns; they pose significant risks to public health, economic stability, and food security. Coastal communities face immediate threats from sea-level rise, while vulnerable regions grapple with the consequences of extreme droughts, floods, and storms. According to recent data, up to 200 million people may be displaced by 2050 due to climate-related pressures (Smith et al., 2023). Addressing these urgent issues requires strategies that are as nuanced as they are comprehensive, focusing on both immediate action and sustainable long-term solutions.

Technological Innovation: Promise and Peril

Technological advancements hold the potential to drive positive change, yet they also introduce new complexities. Artificial intelligence (AI), automation, and biotechnology are reshaping our industries and challenging traditional job structures, raising ethical questions about privacy, equity, and the displacement of human labor. For instance, while AI can improve efficiency in fields like healthcare and logistics, it may also lead to significant job loss in sectors dependent on routine tasks. Balancing technological progress with ethical considerations is crucial. Policymakers, innovators, and communities must work together to ensure that these technologies are developed and applied in ways that benefit society as a whole.

AI, renewable energy, and sustainable urban planning are key areas where innovation can contribute positively. Smart energy grids, for example, can optimize electricity distribution, reducing waste and lowering emissions. Similarly, autonomous vehicles may reduce traffic congestion and improve air quality in urban centers, provided they are integrated thoughtfully into existing transportation systems. These innovations must be coupled with robust social policies and accessible retraining programs to support workers transitioning into new sectors shaped by automation.

Sustainable Practices: Redefining Human Interaction with Nature

Sustainability is no longer an option; it is an imperative. Human civilization must rethink its relationship with natural resources, moving away from extractive models toward regenerative practices. Industries, governments, and individuals must prioritize renewable resources, reduced waste, and environmental restoration. Circular economies, which minimize waste and maximize resource use through recycling and sustainable production, offer promising alternatives to traditional economic models. For example, biodegradable materials and zero-waste manufacturing can reduce our ecological footprint and lessen the burden on waste management systems.

Agriculture, one of the most resource-intensive industries, also holds enormous potential for sustainable transformation. Precision agriculture, which uses data-driven methods to optimize crop yields while minimizing water and chemical usage, can feed growing populations without further degrading the environment. Community-supported agriculture and urban farming initiatives empower communities to produce food locally, reducing transportation emissions and fostering self-sufficiency.

Building Resilient Societies: Community Empowerment and Education

Resilience is key to withstanding future uncertainties, whether they stem from environmental, economic, or social challenges. Building resilience begins at the community level, where individuals are empowered through education, skill-building, and access to essential resources. Community-led initiatives can improve local infrastructure, offer disaster preparedness training, and create resource-sharing networks that reduce vulnerability.

Education: Defining Its True Essence, Purpose, and Empowering Humanity

Education plays a central role in fostering a resilient and adaptable society, yet it is crucial to redefine what education truly entails. Education extends far beyond formal institutions or the accumulation of degrees—whether a diploma, bachelor's degree, PhD, or postdoctoral qualification. It is not merely a credential to display but rather a continuous, lifelong process encompassing both formal and informal learning. True education immerses individuals in an ongoing journey of self-examination, challenging assumptions, and unlearning ingrained beliefs and biases.

The very notion of using terms like "I think" or "I believe" often reveals an attachment to personal biases and limitations. This perspective encourages individuals to shed preconceived notions, continuously striving toward disillusionment and the revelation of truth, which allows them to observe reality with greater mental clarity as they become aware of their own ignorance.

Adopting such an educational mindset cultivates a state of intellectual curiosity and adaptability. It empowers individuals and communities to acknowledge and confront their ignorance collaboratively, building a richer, cumulative understanding over time. By embracing unlearning as a core principle, education transcends mere knowledge acquisition and becomes a lifelong journey of questioning, discovery, and growth.

To prepare future generations to address global challenges, formal and informal education systems must incorporate relevant topics like critical thinking, climate science, sustainability, and digital literacy into their curricula. These subjects equip young people with the knowledge and practical skills needed to navigate complex global issues. However, education must extend beyond these frameworks. Lifelong learning initiatives, especially in fast-evolving fields like artificial intelligence and renewable energy, support continuous skill development, empowering individuals to adapt to shifting job markets and societal needs.

Ultimately, genuine education is not about the acquisition of static knowledge but about nurturing an open mind and a willingness to question and refine one's understanding. Education is not a static endpoint but a dynamic, evolving process that inspires individuals and communities to reach toward deeper awareness and collaborative wisdom. Through the ongoing accumulation of knowledge, education enables us to continuously adjust, adapt, and respond to the demands of an ever-changing world.

Inclusive access to education and resources is critical for resilience. Economic disparities limit opportunities for many individuals, particularly in developing regions, to access the training and tools they need to thrive. By ensuring equitable access to education, healthcare, and employment, societies can build a stronger foundation of resilience and reduce the impact of global inequalities.

Critical Thinking

In the context of formal education—particularly within the structured classroom or lecture hall setting—critical thinking demands a willingness to delve into inquiry that transcends surface-level understanding. At its core, this involves a systematic approach to questioning that begins with "**what**," moves to "**how**," and then reaches the fundamental "**why**" behind any concept, process, or theory. This sequence serves not only to deepen understanding but also to push educators—whether teachers, tutors, tenured professors, or contract faculty—beyond conventional boundaries of knowledge and pedagogy.

When a student's questions lead an educator to the honest admission, "I do not know," a powerful dynamic unfolds: the student and educator embark on a collaborative journey of exploration, one that dismantles traditional hierarchies of knowledge and authority.

In an ideal setting, when a question arises that defies easy answers, the educator—particularly those with tenure, given their role in fostering academic rigor and innovation—should openly acknowledge the question's intelligence. In doing so, the educator validates the student's critical engagement and sets a tone of mutual respect. Importantly, rather than resorting to vague responses, the educator should model humility by saying, "I do not know the answer. I will inquire further and come back with options for us to explore together." This response not only encourages intellectual honesty but also demonstrates a commitment to the learning process as a shared experience rather than a one-way transmission of information.

When students challenge their educators to the point of discomfort—especially in higher education settings—such questions reveal a pivotal truth about learning itself: true education is a process of **unlearning** ingrained beliefs, assumptions, and supposed certainties. It requires students and educators alike to confront their own limitations and biases, embracing the inevitable discomfort that arises when deeply held views are questioned. For educators, this means setting aside any pretense of infallibility and engaging vulnerably with students, acknowledging that learning is an evolving and collaborative journey.

For students, the aim should be to pose questions with respect and clarity, honoring the educator's authority while recognizing that **true authority lies in the ability to admit one's limitations.** Using academic language and maintaining decorum is essential to preserving the learning environment as a dynamic, living ecosystem. This approach underscores a commitment to constructive discourse rather than confrontation; fostering an atmosphere where ideas can thrive, evolve, and interact freely. Such respectful communication allows for diverse perspectives to emerge and be explored, enriching the educational experience for all participants.

However, when an educator dismisses such questions, labeling a student as disruptive or claiming that probing inquiries hinder the learning environment for others, this response can be seen as an evasion rooted in pride rather than pedagogy. **Such a reaction suggests an abuse of authority:** by discouraging genuine inquiry, the educator implicitly exploits their position and authority, prioritizing the preservation of their own image over the educational development of all students.

This behavior by the educator constitutes an abuse of power, as it exploits other students to mask the educator's own excessive pride. One tactic they may use is to single out the inquisitive student, labeling them as "gifted," "genius" or "brighter" than their peers and fabricating narratives that trigger envy, jealousy and resentment among the other students. This exploitation isolates the student who posed the intelligent question, whose inquiry may have already exposed the educator's limitations. Such tactics are timeworn and can be traced back to ancient civilizations, from Sumerian society onward. Both educators and leaders have used these strategies to control groups through the familiar mechanisms of "divide and conquer," stirring up emotions like envy and jealousy to incite division.

These tactics often rely on a form of "relational aggression" that is particularly effective during adolescence, yet remains deeply embedded in the human psyche throughout life. The creation of opposing "political parties" and "interest groups," which capitalize on rivalries and insecurities about who holds the "superior" narrative, reflects this enduring strategy. This manipulation of competitive and comparative emotions is a well-documented method that, rather than fostering peace, harmony, resilience, and unity or understanding, exploits human vulnerabilities for control and influence.

When this happens, the student's power becomes evident—not in undermining the educator's role, but in illuminating the need for humility and adaptability within the academic hierarchy.

Ultimately, the process of learning involves confronting both students' and educators' shared ignorance. True education thrives in a space where questions are uncomfortable, where answers are not readily available, and where intellectual growth requires the dismantling of previous knowledge.

When educators remove the mask of authority and embrace humility, they cultivate a learning environment—a dynamic ecosystem—that fosters resilience, adaptability, and a deep respect for the ongoing journey of discovery. By encouraging unlearning of what we once thought, believed, and imagined we knew, education transcends mere knowledge acquisition. It becomes a transformative force, our "saving grace," guiding us toward deeper understanding and intellectual openness.

The Role of International Cooperation and Collaborative Action

Global challenges require global solutions. Climate change, resource depletion, and technological disruption do not respect national borders. International cooperation, driven by shared goals and mutual accountability, is essential for tackling these issues at scale. Multinational agreements, such as the Paris Agreement on climate change, demonstrate the potential for collaborative action, but these initiatives require consistent commitment and enforcement to be effective.

Collaboration must extend beyond governments to include corporations, NGOs, and individuals. Cross-sector partnerships can drive sustainable development, align economic incentives with environmental goals, and promote research and innovation. Corporations have a responsibility to implement sustainable practices and support global efforts through corporate social responsibility initiatives. NGOs and civil society organizations play a vital role in advocating for policy changes, raising public awareness, and supporting vulnerable communities.

Chapter 8

Envisioning a Collaborative, Harmonious Global Society

The future of human civilization rests on our ability to foster cooperation, mutual respect, and shared progress. This vision requires more than technological innovation or economic growth; it demands a shift in values toward prioritizing human welfare, environmental stewardship, and ethical governance. By fostering a global culture that values sustainability, equity, and empathy, humanity can transcend narrow, self-interested pursuits and work towards a common good.

A harmonious global society is achievable when individuals and communities take responsibility for both their immediate environments and the broader planet. This requires us to be stewards of our shared resources, advocates for justice, and allies in the fight against inequality. Local actions, multiplied across communities, can lead to global transformations that benefit everyone.

Conclusion: Charting a Path to a Sustainable Future

The challenges we face are daunting, but they are not insurmountable. By embracing sustainable practices, ethical innovation, and inclusive governance, human civilization can overcome the obstacles before us. The solutions lie not only in technological advancements but in the way we approach our relationship with the planet and each other. This final chapter calls for action rooted in collaborative responsibility and a vision of a better world. The future of human civilization depends on our willingness to adapt, collaborate, and prioritize the long-term well-being of all life on Earth. By fostering a spirit of cooperation and shared progress, we can build a sustainable and resilient global society that will thrive for generations to come.

As we close this chapter, the path forward is clear: it is time to invest in a civilization that is not only advanced but also ethical, inclusive, and deeply connected to the natural world. In doing so, we create a legacy of resilience, empathy, and stewardship that will define the future of human civilization.

In considering the future of human civilization, it is vital to address the imminent challenges that lie ahead. Climate change, technological innovation, and social resilience are among the most pressing issues we face, each demanding immediate, concerted action. Through the development of sustainable solutions and the responsible application of new technologies, we can steer humanity toward a future characterized by balance, resilience, and inclusivity.

Climate Change and Environmental Responsibility

Climate change remains an urgent, pervasive threat. The evidence is unmistakable: rising global temperatures, melting ice caps, and increasingly unpredictable weather patterns signify a planet under severe stress.

In this context, embracing sustainable practices is no longer a choice; it has become a necessity. Simple shifts—like adopting renewable energy sources, reducing waste through comprehensive recycling programs, and optimizing transportation efficiency—can contribute significantly to lowering our collaborative carbon footprint (Eckstein et al., 2023).

Every individual effort adds up, accumulating to create substantial change over time. Practical steps individuals can take include:

- **Choosing renewable energy** when available.
- **Opting for public transport, carpooling, or biking** to reduce emissions.
- **Minimizing waste** by recycling and supporting companies committed to sustainability.
- **Engaging in community initiatives** that prioritize environmental conservation.

These actions may seem minor on an individual level, yet they carry the potential to catalyze widespread impact when adopted collaboratively.

Harnessing Technology for a Sustainable Future

Technology holds immense potential as both a tool for mitigating climate change and a pathway to sustainable development. Clean energy technologies, such as solar and wind power, are revolutionizing the energy sector. Innovations in battery storage ensure that excess renewable energy can be stored effectively, creating a more consistent supply even when renewable resources fluctuate. Additionally, smart grid technology enhances electricity distribution efficiency, cutting down on waste and increasing reliability.

On a personal scale, individuals can incorporate intelligent home systems that optimize energy use, reducing consumption and lowering utility bills. Electric vehicles (EVs) represent another transformative shift, offering a cleaner alternative to fossil-fuel-powered cars. As EV adoption grows and charging infrastructure becomes more accessible, air pollution and greenhouse gas emissions are expected to decline substantially (IEA, 2022).

Beyond environmental impact, technological advancements are reshaping various sectors. Artificial intelligence (AI) and automation hold promise for enhancing productivity and introducing groundbreaking advancements in fields like healthcare. AI can make diagnostics more accurate and accessible, while autonomous vehicles could reduce traffic accidents and ease urban congestion.

However, these technological shifts come with significant social responsibilities. As automation replaces certain routine jobs, it is crucial to invest in re-skilling and up-skilling programs to equip workers for roles that emerge from these innovations. Inclusivity must also be a priority to prevent underserved communities from being left behind as technology advances. Striking a balance between embracing innovation and fostering workforce resilience is key.

Building Resilient Societies Through Local Empowerment

To effectively address an array of challenges, societies must foster resilience at the local level. Resilient societies are grounded in strong, interconnected communities where individuals support one another in pursuing shared goals. Grassroots movements are central to this model, empowering people to take control of their own futures and create networks of mutual aid and solidarity.

Decentralized, community-based grassroots initiatives form the backbone of resilient societal structures. These communities act as safety nets, ensuring that vulnerable individuals are supported. This approach fosters personal responsibility while recognizing that mutual support is essential. Robust local networks help mitigate societal challenges by empowering individuals and strengthening the community as a whole (Berkes and Berkes, 2021).

In times of crisis, whether due to natural disasters or economic downturns, resilient communities offer swift adaptation and recovery. Their inherent flexibility, coupled with strong interpersonal relationships, provides a foundation for community-driven solutions. Supporting local businesses, participating in communal events, and investing in shared resources can enhance resilience across communities.

Global Collaboration for Shared Progress

To create a harmonious global society, we must embrace international cooperation. Many of the world's most complex problems—such as global health crises and environmental degradation—can only be solved through collaborative action. Working together across borders enables resource pooling, knowledge sharing, and solution development that benefits humanity as a whole.

Effective cooperation stems from mutual respect and understanding. Every nation offers unique strengths and perspectives, which, when combined, can lead to innovative solutions and comprehensive strategies. Individuals can contribute to global harmony by staying informed about international issues, supporting organizations that promote cooperation, and adopting an open-minded approach to cultural diversity (Klingler-Vidra et al., 2023).

The trajectory of human civilization depends on our collaborative ability to adapt, innovate, and collaborate. Through a commitment to sustainable practices, responsible technology use, and community resilience, we can navigate the uncertainties of the future. By working individually and collaboratively, we have the power to build a world where humanity flourishes, guided by values of fairness, responsibility, and mutual support.

The Role of Education in Shaping the Future

Education plays a central role in preparing societies for the future. However, education is not limited to formal credentials like degrees. True education is an ongoing, lifelong process that involves unlearning biases and challenging preconceived notions. Real education fosters intellectual curiosity, humility, and openness to truth, prompting individuals to question what they think they know.

To address global challenges effectively, educational systems must integrate climate science, sustainability, and digital literacy into their curricula. Future generations need these skills to navigate an increasingly complex world. Lifelong learning, particularly in fields like AI and renewable energy, is essential to help individuals adapt to changing job markets and evolving societal needs.

Nurturing Critical Thinking in Education

Critical thinking is an essential component of effective education, particularly in formal academic settings. In classrooms, fostering critical thinking requires encouraging students to ask foundational questions, progressing from "what" and "how" to "why."

When students pose insightful questions, educators should recognize the value of these inquiries, responding with humility when answers are uncertain. Statements like, "I do not know the answer, but I will look into it, and we can learn together," acknowledge the student's curiosity while reinforcing the value of lifelong learning.

This approach not only fosters intellectual growth but also challenges educators to expand their own knowledge. By embracing these moments, teachers create an environment where humility, inquiry, and adaptability are integral to the learning process.

Embracing Empathy and Cultural Sensitivity

Empathy and cultural sensitivity are essential for building a cooperative global society. Direct human connections foster genuine relationships, transcending cultural barriers. Decentralized grassroots initiatives, like community-led festivals and local art projects, facilitate authentic exchanges that nurture mutual respect and understanding.

Additionally, shared values—such as environmental stewardship, economic sustainability, and community health—serve as unifying forces. Community conservation efforts, local economic practices, and wellness programs all offer ways for people to connect meaningfully, reinforcing a sense of collaborative responsibility.

A Call for Evidence-Based Action and Balanced Progress

Moving forward, a commitment to evidence-based approaches is critical for ensuring that our actions are both effective and responsible. Rooting our decisions in empirical data and thoughtful analysis will enable us to address challenges methodically, crafting solutions grounded in reality rather than idealism. This approach ensures that progress is sustainable and inclusive.

In balancing economic growth with human welfare, and promoting individual responsibility alongside communal support, we can build a world marked by resilience, fairness, and shared prosperity. Each of us plays a part in this endeavor. Through individual actions and collaborative efforts, we can create a society where every individual has the opportunity to thrive.

As we face the challenges of the future, let us remain committed to principles of justice, compassion, and adaptability. By focusing on sustainable development, responsible technology use, and robust community structures, we can build a resilient world that values human dignity and collaborative well-being.

Looking toward the future of human civilization, we stand at a critical juncture. The strategies we adopt today will shape the world for generations to come, and to address the challenges ahead—ranging from climate change to technological innovation and social resilience—we must embrace forward-thinking solutions rooted in sustainability and personal responsibility. By envisioning a future where humanity thrives in harmony with the planet, we can begin taking concrete steps toward meaningful progress.

Climate Change: A Call to Action

Climate change is no longer just an environmental issue; it has become a defining human challenge. The air we breathe, the water we drink, and the food we eat are all impacted by the environmental choices we make. Embracing sustainable practices is therefore essential. Each of us can contribute to this effort in meaningful ways, and even small actions can create substantial global impact.

Reducing waste, conserving energy, and supporting renewable energy sources are some simple yet effective ways to reduce our environmental footprint. For instance, opting for public transportation or biking rather than driving can drastically cut carbon emissions. Switching to energy-efficient appliances, choosing eco-friendly products, and minimizing waste through recycling are additional ways to make a significant difference (Ivanova et al., 2020).

Imagine a world where rooftops are covered with solar panels and urban areas are filled with vibrant community gardens. These are not distant dreams but achievable goals within our reach. Solar technology has advanced considerably, making it accessible and affordable for many. Installing solar panels on homes and businesses enables people to harness clean energy, reducing their reliance on fossil fuels.

Furthermore, urban farms transform underutilized spaces into green havens that provide fresh produce, foster biodiversity, and improve air quality. Community support for these initiatives—through local purchases, participation in gardening programs, or even starting a home garden—can amplify their impact.

Technological Innovation: Bridging the Gap to a Sustainable Future

Technology is more than a tool; it is a bridge to a more sustainable world. However, while technological advancement brings potential solutions, it also introduces new challenges. We need to ensure that technology serves both humanity and the environment. Environmentally friendly innovations have the potential to transform industries, increase efficiency, and reduce waste.

Advances in battery technology, for example, are making electric vehicles (EVs) a viable alternative to traditional cars. This shift not only reduces greenhouse gas emissions but also lowers dependence on fossil fuels. Likewise, smart home technology can optimize energy consumption, leading to reduced household carbon footprints (Sovacool et al., 2021).

Artificial intelligence (AI) also presents promising avenues for sustainable progress. AI applications can monitor and optimize energy usage, forecast and manage natural disasters, and improve agricultural practices to enhance food security. By incorporating AI in these ways, we can ensure that our actions are beneficial both for individuals and society as a whole. However, the adoption of AI also raises ethical considerations, requiring us to balance technological benefits with workforce resilience and inclusivity.

Balancing Economic Growth with Human Welfare

Economic progress should not come at the expense of human health and welfare. Instead, it should enhance them. The key lies in fostering entrepreneurship and innovation that emphasize both profit and purpose.

Supporting startups and businesses that prioritize sustainable practices can drive positive change while also creating economic opportunities. By investing in companies that align with ethical values, promoting conscious consumption, and advocating for corporate responsibility, individuals can help reshape the economy to serve both people and the planet (Mazzucato and Dibb, 2023).

Education as a Pillar of Resilience

Education is fundamental to building a resilient society. True education extends beyond formal institutions; it involves a lifelong commitment to learning, critical thinking, and personal growth. Educational systems must evolve to nurture not only academic skills but also creativity, adaptability, and a sense of responsibility. By integrating climate science, sustainability, and digital literacy into curricula, educational institutions can equip future generations with the knowledge and skills necessary to address global challenges.

Continuous education through online courses, community learning centers, and workshops can provide accessible avenues for skill development. Encouraging lifelong learning allows individuals to adapt to shifting circumstances, preparing them for new opportunities and roles in a rapidly changing world.

Reimagining Health Care for Holistic Well-being

Our current health care systems often fall short of addressing the full spectrum of human health needs. Integrating preventive care and mental health services with traditional medical approaches can lead to healthier, more resilient communities. Individuals also play a role in taking responsibility for their health through balanced diets, regular exercise, mindfulness practices, and preventive check-ups. These personal actions contribute to overall well-being and help create communities where health is prioritized.

Building Resilient Societies through Community Empowerment

Empowering individuals within their communities is key to addressing a diverse range of challenges effectively. Grassroots movements, rooted in decentralized, community-based action, are instrumental in fostering resilience. These movements enable people to take control of their circumstances, create networks of mutual aid, and build solidarity.

Strong local communities provide safety nets for their members and foster a sense of mutual care. This model promotes personal responsibility while acknowledging that everyone may need support at some point. Community networks offer this support, creating balance and empowering individuals and neighborhoods alike (Berkes and Berkes, 2021). In times of adversity, such as natural disasters or economic downturns, resilient communities adapt and recover quickly due to their inherent flexibility and strong interpersonal bonds.

Supporting local businesses, engaging in communal activities, and investing in shared resources all serve to reinforce community resilience, creating a foundation upon which society can flourish.

Cooperation and Shared Progress

A harmonious global society is not built on competition but on collaboration. When individuals from different backgrounds and cultures work together to share knowledge, skills, and experiences, they create synergies that drive mutual growth. Participating in local initiatives, joining global networks, and fostering cross-cultural exchanges can strengthen bonds, promote understanding, and inspire innovation.

Envision a future where bustling cities are powered by renewable energy, green spaces and urban farms are commonplace, and technology is seamlessly integrated into daily life to support convenience and sustainability. Picture a world where education empowers individuals, health care embraces holistic well-being, and diversity is celebrated as a strength. In this vision, resilience defines society—communities adapt to change with agility, leveraging technology and sustainability to meet challenges head-on. Individuals take responsibility for their actions, and their collaborative efforts ripple outward, impacting the world positively for generations to come.

By embracing evidence-driven solutions and prioritizing human welfare, we can create a world where progress is measured not only in economic terms but also in the well-being and happiness of every individual (Sachs et al., 2023).

A Call to Action

As we look to the future, remember that each of us has a role to play. The choices we make today will shape the world of tomorrow. Let us commit to sustainable practices, embrace technological innovation, and foster resilient societies. By working together, we can build a harmonious global community where humanity not only survives but thrives, empowered by individuality and strengthened by collaborative action.

In this pursuit, let us remain grounded in principles of fairness, responsibility, and shared prosperity. As we face the challenges of the future, may we stay committed to evidence-based approaches and thoughtful analysis. By balancing economic growth with human welfare and combining personal responsibility with community support, we lay the groundwork for a just, resilient world where everyone has the opportunity to flourish.

Embracing a Future Rooted in Individual Strengths

As we stand at the threshold of the future, envisioning the paths our civilization might take, it becomes clear that our actions today are the foundations of tomorrow's world. The urgent challenges of climate change and rapid technological innovation are interwoven threads in the fabric of a complex global landscape. By embracing innovative and sustainable solutions, we have the opportunity to build a resilient and harmonious society—one that thrives by adapting to change and fostering balance with our planet and its evolving needs.

Climate change, as underscored, presents an urgent call to action. Our environmental footprint affects every facet of life, from the air we breathe to the food we consume. Embracing renewable energy sources, reducing waste, and promoting sustainable practices are essential steps toward mitigating this global threat. On an individual level, small adjustments—such as choosing energy-efficient appliances—can collaboratively make a substantial impact that resonates across communities and nations.

Technological innovation holds extraordinary potential to redefine our approach to today's most pressing challenges. With advancements in medical sciences, genetics, nanotechnology, electric vehicles, clean energy, and the transformative power of Artificial Intelligence driven by quantum computing, our world stands poised for unprecedented growth.

These innovations unlock previously unimaginable pathways to a sustainable and efficient future. Achieving this vision requires a thoughtful balance of progress with ethical considerations, along with a commitment to individual, communal, and social responsibility.

Initiatives focused on reskilling and upskilling empower individuals to embrace new opportunities, while ensuring inclusive access to technology fosters widespread, equitable benefits. This approach cultivates a competitive yet harmonious balance within each individual and across communities, fostering a life-affirming environment of peace, health, well-being, and equilibrium.

Such efforts equally uphold the health and well-being of individuals and communities, rooted in an inseparable unity—a family bound by the shared destiny of the human species. By harnessing the power of innovation together, we can build a future that uplifts and serves us all.

Building resilient individuals, communities, and societies—beginning precisely in that priority sequence—starts with fostering strong, supportive networks united by shared goals. Grassroots movements and decentralized initiatives empower individuals to establish solidarity and mutual aid, offering invaluable support in times of adversity. By nurturing these connections, we pave the way for a balanced and interconnected society, one capable of thriving in harmonious symbiosis and overcoming diverse challenges.

Looking ahead, cooperation and shared progress are paramount. Through the power of cumulative knowledge, collaboration enables and empowers us to pool resources and insights, addressing challenges at every level—individual, family, community, local, regional, national, and global—in that precise sequence, with amplified effectiveness and impact.

Through joint efforts, we can achieve groundbreaking innovations and craft holistic strategies that uplift both communities and humanity as a whole. Each individual and community brings unique strengths, and together, these perspectives can illuminate a path toward a brighter, more resilient future.

Together, we have the opportunity to shape a future that reflects the best of human potential. By committing to sustainable practices, ethical innovation, and the nurturing of strong, resilient individuals, communities, nations, and the world—in that precise priority sequence—we can confidently and purposefully forge a path through the challenges that lie ahead.

Every choice we make today, grounded in data-driven strategies and thoughtful analysis—yet careful to avoid transforming science and data analysis into a new dogmatic belief system, recognizing them solely as tools—strengthens our ability to build a thriving and sustainable world for generations to come.

Let us embrace these guiding principles, knowing that each step forward brings us closer to a world where humanity flourishes in harmony with our environment and with one another. Moving forward, let's take action with hope and determination, understanding that our individual efforts are the seeds of a resilient, vibrant and harmonious tomorrow.

References

Aboujaoude, E., Gega, L., Parish, M.B. and Hilty, D.M., 2022. Editorial: Digital interventions in mental health: Current status and future directions. Frontiers in Psychiatry, 13, p.869590.

Adger, W.N., Quinn, T., Lorenzoni, I., Murphy, C. and Sweeney, J., 2020. Changing social contracts in climate-change adaptation. Nature Climate Change, 10(7), pp. 611-616.

Alaimo, K. and Tong, S.T., 2020. "If I can't have you, no one can": How targets and romantic rivals communicate about stalking on social media. New Media & Society, 22(7), pp.1237-1256.

Ansell, C. and Gash, A., 2021. Collaborative governance in theory and practice. Journal of Public Administration Research and Theory, 31(4), pp.841-857.

Avelino, F., Dumitru, A., Longhurst, N., Wittmayer, J., Hielscher, S., Weaver, P., Cipolla, C., Afonso, R., Kunze, I., Dorland, J. and Elle, M., 2020. Translocal empowerment in transformative social innovation networks. European Planning Studies, 28(5), pp.955-977.

Bai, C., Dallasega, P., Orzes, G. and Sarkis, J., 2020. Industry 4.0 technologies assessment: A sustainability perspective. International Journal of Production Economics, 229, p.107776.

Bai, X., Dawson, R.J., Ürge-Vorsatz, D., Delgado, G.C., Barau, A.S., Dhakal, S., Dodman, D., Leonardsen, L., Masson-Delmotte, V.,

Roberts, D.C. and Schultz, S., 2022. Six research priorities for cities and climate change. Nature, 555(7694), pp.23-25.

Batson, C.D., Ahmad, N.Y. and Lishner, D.A., 2022. Empathy and altruism. In The Oxford handbook of positive psychology (3rd ed.). Oxford University Press.

Bavel, J.J.V., Baicker, K., Boggio, P.S., Capraro, V., Cichocka, A., Cikara, M., Crockett, M.J., Crum, A.J., Douglas, K.M., Druckman, J.N. and Drury, J., 2023. Using social and behavioural science to support COVID-19 pandemic response. Nature Human Behaviour, 7(1), pp.30-44.

Berkes, F. and Berkes, M.K., 2021. Community-based conservation in a globalized world: Linking theory and practice. Annual Review of Environment and Resources, 46, pp.93-116.

Berkes, F. and Ross, H., 2023. Community resilience: Toward an integrated approach. Society & Natural Resources, 36(1), pp.1-16.

Bhattacharyya, R., Ghosh, B.N. and Nath, S. eds., 2022. Handbook of Community Well-Being Research. Springer Nature.

Bianchi, M. and Ginelli, A., 2023. Grassroots innovations as drivers for sustainability transitions: A systematic literature review. Environmental Innovation and Societal Transitions, 46, p.100717.

Biekart, K. and Fowler, A., 2021. Ownership dynamics in local multi-stakeholder initiatives. Third World Quarterly, 42(1), pp.1-20.

Bietti, L.M., Tilston, O. and Bangerter, A., 2019. Storytelling as adaptive collective sensemaking. Topics in cognitive science, 11(4), pp.710-732.

Bilandzic, H. and Busselle, R., 2021. Narrative persuasion. In The Handbook of Communication Science and Biology (pp. 351-363). Routledge, New York.

Bloom, P., 2021. The sweet spot: The pleasures of suffering and the search for meaning. Random House.

Bozeman, B. and Feeney, M.K., 2023. Public Values and Public Interest: Counterbalancing Economic Individualism. Georgetown University Press.

Campana, P. and Varese, F., 2023. Organized Crime: A Very Short Introduction. Oxford University Press.

Cinelli, M., De Francisci Morales, G., Galeazzi, A., Quattrociocchi, W. and Starnini, M., 2021. The echo chamber effect on social media. Proceedings of the National Academy of Sciences, 118(9), p.e2023301118.

Counted, V., Pargament, K.I., Bechara, A.O., Joynt, S. and Cowden, R.G., 2022. Hope and well-being in vulnerable contexts during the

COVID-19 pandemic: does religious coping matter? The Journal of Positive Psychology, 17(1), pp.70-81.

Counted, V., Possamai, A. and Meade, T., 2020. Relational spirituality and quality of life 2007 to 2017: an integrative research review. Health and Quality of Life Outcomes, 18(1), pp.1-18.

Cremin, T., Flewitt, R., Mardell, B. and Swann, J. eds., 2018. Storytelling in early childhood: Enriching language, literacy and classroom culture. Routledge, London.

Creutzig, F., Niamir, L., Bai, X., Callaghan, M., Cullen, J., Díaz-José, J., Figueroa, M., Grubler, A., Lamb, W.F., Leip, A. and Masanet, E., 2023. Demand-side solutions to climate change mitigation consistent with high levels of well-being. Nature Climate Change, 13(1), pp.36-46.

Crow, D. and Jones, M., 2018. Narratives as tools for influencing policy change. Policy & Politics, 46(2), pp.217-234.

De Weger, E., Van Vooren, N.J.E., Drewes, H.W., Luijkx, K.G. and Baan, C.A., 2023. Achieving successful community engagement: a rapid realist review. BMC Health Services Research, 23(1), p.48.

Decety, J. and Yoder, K.J., 2021. The emerging social neuroscience of human-animal interaction. Trends in Cognitive Sciences, 25(1), pp.1-12.

Delli Carpini, M.X., 2020. Civic engagement. In Oxford Research Encyclopedia of Politics. Oxford University Press.

Dunbar, R.I.M., 2022. The evolution of social complexity. Philosophical Transactions of the Royal Society B, 377(1845), p.20200319.

Eckstein, D., Künzel, V., Schäfer, L. and Winges, M., 2023. Global Climate Risk Index 2021. Germanwatch, Bonn.

Economist Impact, 2023. Climate tech: bridging the gap between innovation and impact. [online] Available at: <https://impact.economist.com/sustainability/net-zero-and-energy/climate-tech-bridging-the-gap-between-innovation-and-impact> [Accessed 13 July 2024].

Enarsson, D., Hinton, J.B. and Borgström, S., 2024. Grassroots initiatives transforming cities toward post-growth futures: Insights from the collaborative economy movement in Gothenburg, Sweden. Journal of Cleaner Production, 440, p.130880.

Firth, J., Torous, J., Stubbs, B., Firth, J.A., Steiner, G.Z., Smith, L., Alvarez-Jimenez, M., Gleeson, J., Vancampfort, D., Armitage, C.J. and Sarris, J., 2019. The "online brain": how the Internet may be changing our cognition. World Psychiatry, 18(2), pp.119-129.

Fleer, M. and Hammer, M., 2013. Emotions in Imaginative Situations: The Valued Place of Fairytales for Supporting Emotion Regulation. Mind, Culture, and Activity, 20(3), pp.240-259.

Folke, C., Polasky, S., Rockström, J., Galaz, V., Westley, F., Lamont, M., Scheffer, M., Österblom, H., Carpenter, S.R., Chapin III, F.S. and Seto, K.C., 2022. Our future in the Anthropocene biosphere: Global sustainability and resilient societies. Ambio, 51(9), pp.1964-1979.

Frey, C.B. and Osborne, M.A., 2017. The future of employment: How susceptible are jobs to computerisation? Technological forecasting and social change, 114, pp.254-280.

Fung, A. and Wright, E.O., 2023. Deepening Democracy: Institutional Innovations in Empowered Participatory Governance. Verso Books.

Ganz, M. and McKenna, E., 2022. Organizing: People, Power, Change. Oxford University Press.

Geels, F.W., Sovacool, B.K., Schwanen, T. and Sorrell, S., 2020. The socio-technical dynamics of low-carbon transitions. Joule, 4(9), pp. 2066-2090.

Gilkey, R. and Kilts, C., 2023. Cognitive Fitness: A New Frontier for Executive Performance. Harvard Business Review, 101(4), pp.120-129.

Gond, J.P., El Akremi, A., Swaen, V. and Babu, N., 2021. The psychological microfoundations of corporate social responsibility: A person-centric systematic review. Journal of Organizational Behavior, 42(2), pp.144-167.

Government of Canada, 2019. A Guide to Establishing and Maintaining a Psychological Health and Safety Management System. [online] Available at: https://www.canada.ca/en/government/publicservice/wellness-inclusion-diversity-public-service/health-wellness-public-servants/mental-health-workplace/guide-psychological-health-safety-management-system.html [Accessed 15 July 2024].

Grimes, M.K., 2022. Myth, magic and meaning in Harry Potter. Routledge, New York.

Han, H., Ballard, P.J. and Choi, Y.J., 2021. Links between moral identity and political purpose during emerging adulthood. Journal of Moral Education, 50(2), pp.166-184.

IEA, 2022. Global EV Outlook 2022: Securing Supplies for an Electric Future. International Energy Agency, Paris.

International Renewable Energy Agency (IRENA), 2021. Renewable Energy Statistics 2021. Abu Dhabi: IRENA.

IPCC, 2021. Climate Change 2021: The Physical Science Basis. Contribution of Working Group I to the Sixth Assessment Report of the Intergovernmental Panel on Climate Change. Cambridge University Press, Cambridge, United Kingdom and New York, NY, USA.

Itzchakov, G. and Kluger, A.N., 2022. The power of listening in helping people change. Annual Review of Psychology, 73, pp.313-337.

Ivanova, D., Barrett, J., Wiedenhofer, D., Macura, B., Callaghan, M. and Creutzig, F., 2020. Quantifying the potential for climate change mitigation of consumption options. Environmental Research Letters, 15(9), p.093001.

Jepson, A. and Clarke, A. eds., 2022. Managing and Developing Community Festivals and Events. Routledge.

Jepson, A. and Stadler, R., 2024. Reimagining Community Festivals and Events: Critical and Interdisciplinary Perspectives. Routledge.

Jones, S.M. and Kahn, J., 2020. The evidence base for how learning happens: A consensus on social, emotional, and academic development. American Educator, 43(4), pp.16-21.

Kapucu, N. and Garayev, V., 2021. Designing, managing, and sustaining functionally collaborative emergency management networks. The American Review of Public Administration, 51(6), pp.436-458.

Karremans, J.C., Krahmer, E., and Ouwerkerk, J.W., 2020. Interpersonal Acceptance and Rejection in the Digital Age: A Meta-Analysis. Computers in Human Behavior, 113, p.106507.

Keating, D.M. and Jarvenpaa, S.L., 2022. Words matter: communicating effectively in the new global office. MIT Sloan Management Review, 63(2), pp.1-4.

Keating, D.M., Totenhagen, C.J., Faw, M.H. and Lefebvre, L.E., 2023. Positive Communication Processes in Close Relationships. In Positive Communication in Health and Wellness (pp. 17-34). New York: Routledge.

Khoury, B., Dionne, F. and Grégoire, S., 2023. The Role of Self-Compassion in Fostering Positive Interpersonal Relationships: A Systematic Review and Meta-Analysis. Mindfulness, 14(4), pp.731-748.

Kiecolt-Glaser, J.K., Wilson, S.J., Bailey, M.L., Andridge, R., Peng, J., Jaremka, L.M., Fagundes, C.P., Malarkey, W.B., Laskowski, B. and Belury, M.A., 2022. Marital distress, depression, and a leaky gut: Translocation of bacterial endotoxin as a pathway to inflammation. Psychoneuroendocrinology, 138, p.105607.

Klingler-Vidra, R., Engel, S., Paranamana, N. and Crack, A.M., 2023. Global problem-solving approaches: How UNDP and USAID navigate complexity. Global Policy, 14(2), pp.209-221.

Knutson, B. and Huettel, S.A., 2021. Linking brain and behavior in value-based decision-making: A citation network analysis. NeuroImage, 235, p.118031. Available at: https://www.sciencedirect.com/science/article/pii/S1053811921002640 [Accessed 18 July 2024].

Krasny, M.E. and Tidball, K.G., 2023. Civic Ecology: Adaptation and Transformation from the Ground Up. MIT Press.

Kreplin, U., Farias, M. and Brazil, I.A., 2021. The limited prosocial effects of meditation: A systematic review and meta-analysis. Scientific Reports, 11(1), p.5144.

Kreuz, R., & Roberts, R. (2019). *Proxemics 101: Understanding Personal Space Across Cultures.* The MIT Press Reader.

Krumrei-Mancuso, E.J., 2023. Intellectual humility: A theoretically grounded and empirically validated virtue. In The Psychology of Humility (pp. 101-124). Routledge.

Krumrei-Mancuso, E.J., Haggard, M.C., LaBouff, J.P. and Rowatt, W.C., 2020. Links between intellectual humility and acquiring knowledge. The Journal of Positive Psychology, 15(2), pp.155-170.

Liu, D., Liu, X., and Wu, S., 2020. A Literature Review of Diffusion of Responsibility Phenomenon. Atlantis Press. Available at: [PDF] A Literature Review of Diffusion of Responsibility Phenomenon.

Lugmayr, A., Sutinen, E., Suhonen, J., Sedano, C.I., Hlavacs, H. and Montero, C.S., 2022. Serious storytelling–a first definition and review. Multimedia tools and applications, 81, pp.31313-31341.

Lugmayr, A., Sutinen, E., Suhonen, J., Sedano, C.I., Hlavacs, H. and Montero, C.S. eds., 2023. Narrative and Storytelling in Digital Environments. Cham: Springer International Publishing.

Lugmayr, A., Sutinen, E., Suhonen, J., Sedano, C.I., Hlavacs, H. and Montero, C.S. eds., 2022. Narrative and Storytelling in Digital Environments. Cham: Springer International Publishing.

Lugmayr, A., Sutinen, E., Suhonen, J., Sedano, C.I., Hlavacs, H. and Montero, C.S., 2023. Serious storytelling: Narrative and game-based learning in the digital age. International Journal of Serious Games, 10(1), pp.5-25.

Lund, N.F., Cohen, S.A. and Scarles, C., 2018. The power of social media storytelling in destination branding. Journal of destination marketing & management, 8, pp.271-280.

Manzini, E. and Rizzo, F., 2021. Small projects/large changes: Participatory design as an open participated process. CoDesign, 17(1), pp.4-20.

Marston, C., Renedo, A., Nyaaba, G.N., Machiyama, K., Tapsoba, P. and Cleland, J., 2023. Community engagement in COVID-19 responses: Evidence from low-and middle-income countries. Health Policy and Planning, 38(1), pp.73-83.

Mauser, W., Klepper, G., Zabel, F., Delzeit, R., Hank, T., Putzenlechner, B. and Calzadilla, A., 2020. Different approaches to integrate stakeholder perspectives in complex sustainability research: The case of future-oriented transdisciplinary scenario development. Sustainability, 12(6), p.2499.

Mazzucato, M. and Dibb, G., 2023. Redefining value creation for a sustainable and inclusive economy. Nature Sustainability, 6(3), pp.238-246.

Mercier, H. and Sperber, D., 2020. Not born yesterday: The science of who we trust and what we believe. Princeton University Press.

Mesoudi, A., 2021. Cultural evolution: How Darwinian theory can explain human culture and synthesize the social sciences. 2nd ed. Chicago: University of Chicago Press.

Mihaylov, N.L. and Perkins, D.D., 2023. Revisiting place-based environmental action: Grassroots stewardship, community organizing, and ecology of civic action. Journal of Environmental Psychology, 85, p.101921.

Moieni, M. and Eisenberger, N.I., 2020. Effects of inflammation on social processes and implications for health. Annals of the New York Academy of Sciences, 1457(1), pp.5-18.

Mufwene, S.S., 2021. Language evolution: From theory to history. In The Cambridge Handbook of Historical Syntax (pp. 351-376). Cambridge University Press.

Mulindwa, C., 2024. Celebrating World IP Day 2024: Climate Change Innovations for a Sustainable Future. [online] Available at: <https://cipit.org/celebrating-world-ip-day-2024-climate-change-innovations-for-a-sustainable-future/> [Accessed 13 July 2024].

Murray, J.H., 2018. Hamlet on the Holodeck: The Future of Narrative in Cyberspace. Cambridge: MIT Press.

Nagels, A., Kircher, T., Steines, M., Grosvald, M. and Straube, B., 2013. A brief self-rating scale for the assessment of individual differences in gesture perception and production. Cognitive Processing, 14(4), pp.371-380.

National Research Council of Canada (NRC), 2022. Several perspectives on Canada's technology future - 2030–35. [online] Available at: <https://nrc.canada.ca/en/corporate/planning-reporting/horizon-several-perspectives-canadas-technology-future-2030-35> [Accessed 13 July 2024].

Nisa, C.F., Bélanger, J.J., Schumpe, B.M. and Faller, D.G., 2019. Meta-analysis of randomised controlled trials testing behavioural interventions to promote household action on climate change. Nature Communications, 10(1), pp.1-13.

Niu, L., Behar-Horenstein, L.S. and Garvan, C.W., 2023. Promoting critical thinking skills in online learning environments: A systematic review. Computers & Education, 188, p.104564.

Oc, B., Moore, C., Bashshur, M.R., Koopman, J., Mesdaghinia, S. and Aime, F., 2022. Humble leadership: A review, synthesis, and future research agenda. Journal of Management, 48(6), pp.1507-1542.

Page, S.E., 2020. The diversity bonus: How great teams pay off in the knowledge economy. Princeton University Press.

Paradies, Y., Priest, N., Truong, M., Gupta, A., Pieterse, A., Kelaher, M. and Gee, G., 2021. Racism as a determinant of health: A protocol for conducting a systematic review and meta-analysis. Systematic Reviews, 10(1), pp.1-12.

Pettigrew, T.F. and Tropp, L.R., 2021. When groups meet: The dynamics of intergroup contact. Psychology Press.

Pleyers, G., 2020. The Pandemic is a battlefield. Social movements in the COVID-19 lockdown. Journal of Civil Society, 16(4), pp.295-312.

Pratscher, S.D., Wood, P.K., King, L.A. and Bettencourt, B.A., 2019. Interpersonal mindfulness: Scale development and initial construct validation. Mindfulness, 10(6), pp.1044-1061.

Purzycki, B.G., Ross, C.T., Apicella, C., Atkinson, Q.D., Cohen, E., McNamara, R.A., Willard, A.K., Xygalatas, D., Norenzayan, A. and Henrich, J., 2022. Moralistic gods, extended prosociality, and religious disagreement. Philosophical Transactions of the Royal Society B, 377(1843), p.20200316.

Rao, D., Elshafei, A., Nguyen, M., Hatzenbuehler, M.L., Frey, S. and Go, V.F., 2021. A systematic review of multi-level stigma interventions: state of the science and future directions. BMC medicine, 19(1), pp.1-11.

Ren, S., Luthans, F., Zhu, Y. and Li, J., 2022. Leader humility and employee voice: A moderated mediation model of follower perceived organizational support and leader–member exchange. Journal of Leadership & Organizational Studies, 29(2), pp.163-177.

ResearchGate, 2024. Effects of technological innovations on climate change. [online] Available at: <https://www.researchgate.net/publication/379449336_EFFECTS_OF_TECHNOLOGICAL_INNOVATIONS_ON_CLIMATE_CHANGE> [Accessed 13 July 2024].

Rettberg, S., 2019. Electronic literature. Cambridge: Polity Press.

Reysen, S. and Katzarska-Miller, I., 2021. Global Citizenship: Perspectives of a World Community. Springer Nature.

Ribot, J.C., 2002. Democratic decentralization of natural resources: institutionalizing popular participation. World Resources Institute, Washington, DC.

Riedl, M.O., 2021. Human-centered artificial intelligence and machine learning. Human Behavior and Emerging Technologies, 3(2), pp.155-168.

Rosenbaum, M.S. and Rohn, E., 2021. How to improve communication between customers and frontline employees: A transformative service research perspective. Journal of Services Marketing, 35(6), pp.795-808.

Ryan, R.M. and Deci, E.L., 2020. Intrinsic and extrinsic motivation from a self-determination theory perspective: Definitions, theory, practices, and future directions. Contemporary Educational Psychology, 61, p.101860.

Sachs, J.D., Kroll, C., Lafortune, G., Fuller, G. and Woelm, F., 2023. Sustainable Development Report 2023. Cambridge: Cambridge University Press.

Seyfang, G. and Smith, A., 2022. Grassroots innovations for sustainable development: Towards a new research and policy agenda. Environmental Politics, 31(2), pp.295-314.

Shackleford, K.E. and Vinney, C., 2020. Story and Identity: How Stories Influence Who We Are. In: Finding Truth in Fiction: What Fan Culture Gets Right--and Why it's Good to Get Lost in a Story. Oxford: Oxford University Press. Available at: https://academic.oup.com/book/33646/chapter-abstract/288175716 [Accessed 18 July 2024].

Shin, L.M. and Liberzon, I., 2023. The neurocircuitry of fear, stress, and anxiety disorders. Neuropsychopharmacology, 48(1), pp.142-156.

Sloan, R.J., 2020. Artificial intelligence in interactive digital narrative. In Interactive Digital Narrative (pp. 256-270). Routledge, London.

Smith, J. and Smythe, R., 2022. Grassroots Movements and External Influence: Navigating Authenticity in Community Initiatives. Journal of Community Development, 45(3), pp.345-360.

Smith, J., Brown, L., and Johnson, M., 2023. Ethical Leadership and Long-Term Societal Impact. Journal of Social and Behavioral Sciences, 58(3), pp.245-260.

Smith, J., Johnson, A. and Brown, M., 2023. Navigating the Anthropocene: Integrating Climate Action and Responsible Innovation. Nature Sustainability, 6(4), pp.321-330.

Sonnentag, S. and Bayer, U.V., 2022. Detachment from work: A diary study on leisure-time experiences, sleep quality, and their role in employees' work engagement and self-reported work performance. Journal of Occupational and Organizational Psychology, 95(1), pp.197-222.

Sovacool, B.K., Hess, D.J., Amir, S., Geels, F.W., Hirsh, R., Medina, L.R., Miller, C., Palavicino, C.A., Phadke, R., Ryghaug, M. and Schot, J., 2021. Sociotechnical agendas: Reviewing future directions for energy and climate research. Energy Research & Social Science, 70, p.101617.

Spataro, S.E. and Bloch, J., 2021. "Can You Hear Me?": A Meta-Analysis of the Effects of Active Listening. Journal of Management, 47(8), pp.2021-2048.

Stocker, E., Englert, C., Seiler, R. and Schmid, J., 2021. Mindfulness and self-control in sport and exercise: A systematic review. International Review of Sport and Exercise Psychology, 14(1), pp.208-239.

Šūmane, S., Ortiz-Miranda, D. and Pinto-Correia, T., 2021. Small farms' values and ecosystems services in European landscapes. Land Use Policy, 107, p.105442.

Tormos-Aponte, F. and García-López, G.A., 2022. Polycentric governance and power in environmental policy-making. Environmental Policy and Governance, 32(1), pp.55-67.

United Nations, 2022. The Sustainable Development Goals Report 2022. New York: United Nations Publications.

Van Cappellen, P., Edwards, M.E., Fredrickson, B.L., and Saroglou, V., 2021. Upward spirals of positive emotions and spirituality: Exploring dynamic reciprocal links between spiritual practices, positive emotions, and well-being. Journal of Personality and Social Psychology, 120(2), pp.494-514.

Vertovec, S., 2021. The social organization of difference. Ethnic and Racial Studies, 44(8), pp.1273-1295.

Vinuesa, R., Azizpour, H., Leite, I., Balaam, M., Dignum, V., Domisch, S., Felländer, A., Langhans, S.D., Tegmark, M. and Fuso Nerini, F., 2020. The role of artificial intelligence in achieving the Sustainable Development Goals. Nature Communications, 11(1), p.233.

Vorderer, P. and Kohring, M., 2023. Digital well-being: Boundaries and balance in mediatized worlds. New Media & Society, 25(3), pp.611-629.

Vorderer, P. and Kohring, M., 2023. Digital well-being: Boundaries and balance in mediatized worlds. New Media & Society, 25(3), pp.611-629.

Waddock, S., 2023. Narrative, Storytelling, and Systems Change. Business & Society, 62(3), pp.491-529.

Wielgosz, J., Goldberg, S.B., Kral, T.R., Dunne, J.D. and Davidson, R.J., 2023. Mindfulness meditation and psychopathology. Annual Review of Clinical Psychology, 19, pp.225-253.

Wynes, S. and Nicholas, K.A., 2017. The climate mitigation gap: education and government recommendations miss the most effective individual actions. Environmental Research Letters, 12(7), p.074024.

Yeboah, S.A., 2023. Balancing Growth and Green: Strategies for Sustainable Development in Developing Economies. MPRA Paper No. 118180, posted 03 Aug 2023 15:37 UTC. Available at: https://mpra.ub.uni-muenchen.de/118180/1/Balancing%20Growth%20and%20Green%20FOR%20MPRA%20FINAL.pdf [Accessed 13 July 2024].

Zajko, V. and Hoyle, H. eds., 2021. A handbook to the reception of classical mythology. Hoboken: John Wiley & Sons.

Zajko, V. and Hoyle, H. eds., 2022. A handbook to the reception of classical mythology. John Wiley & Sons.

Zipes, J., 2021. The irresistible fairy tale: The cultural and social history of a genre. Princeton University Press.

Zmigrod, L., Eisenberg, I.W., Bissett, P.G., Robbins, T.W. and Poldrack, R.A., 2023. A cognitive phenotype for intellectual humility. Nature Human Behaviour, 7(1), pp.19-31.

www.ingramcontent.com/pod-product-compliance
Lightning Source LLC
Chambersburg PA
CBHW060531100426
42743CB00009B/1493